CONCILIUM

MONOTHEISM

CLAUDE GEFFRÉ AND
JEAN-PIERRE JOSSUA

CONCILIUM

Religion in the Eighties

CONCILIUM

Editorial Directors

General Secretariat: Prins Bernhardstraat 2, 6521 AB Nijmegen, The Netherlands

Concilium 177 (1/1985): Fundamental Theology

CONCILIUM

List of Members

Advisory Committee: Fundamental Theology

Directors:

Claude Geffré OP	Paris	France
Jean-Pierre Jossua OP	Paris	France

Members:

Alfonso Alvarez Bolado ST	Madrid	Spain
Maurice Boutin	Montreal, Quebec	Canada
Bertrand de Clercq OP	Louvain	Belgium
Joseph Comblin	Recife	Brazil
Etienne Cornélis	Nijmegen	The Netherlands
Richard Cote OMI	Brighton, Ma.	USA
Iring Fetscher	Frankfurt/Main	West Germany
Francis Fiorenza	Hyattsville, Md.	USA
José Fondevila SJ	Barcelona	Spain
Heinrich Fries	Munich	West Germany
Pierre Gisel	Lausanne	Switzerland
Matthew Lamb	Milwaukee, Wis.	USA
Bernard Lauret	Paris	France
Italo Mancini	Urbino	Italy
Sally McFague	Nashville, Ten.	USA
Andreas van Melsen	Nijmegen	The Netherlands
Johann-Baptist Metz	Münster	West Germany
Christopher Mooney SJ	Fairfield, Conn.	USA
Francis O'Farrell SJ	Rome	Italy
Raimundo Panikkar	Santa Barbara, Cal.	USA
Helmuth Rolfes	Bielefeld	West Germany
Ludwig Rütti	Lengerich	West Germany
Giuseppe Ruggieri	Catania	Italy
Juan-Carlos Scannone SJ	San Miguel	Argentine
Norbert Schiffers	Aachen	West Germany
Heinz Schlette	Bonn	West Germany
Jon Sobrino	San Salvador	El Salvador
Robert Spaemann	Stuttgart-Botnang	West Germany
David Tracy	Chicago, Ill.	USA
Roberto Tucci SJ	Vatican City	Italy
Jan Walgrave OP	Louvain	Belgium

MONOTHEISM

Edited by
Claude Geffré
and
Jean-Pierre Jossua

English Language Editor
Marcus Lefébure

T. & T. CLARK LTD
Edinburgh

February 1985
T. & T. Clark Ltd, 36 George Street, Edinburgh EH2 2LQ
ISBN: 0 567 30057 9

ISSN: 0010-5236

Typeset by C. R. Barber & Partners (Highlands) Ltd, Fort William
Printed by Page Brothers (Norwich) Ltd

Concilium: Published February, April, June, August, October, December.
Subscriptions 1985: UK: £19.95 (including postage and packing); USA: US$40.00
(including air mail postage and packing); Canada: Canadian$50.00 (including air mail
postage and packing); other countries: £19.95 (including postage and packing).

CONTENTS

Part III
Present-Day Questions

Editorial

WHY DEVOTE an issue of *Concilium* to the question of monotheism? Some people will remind us that monotheism is an unshaken constant of Catholic theology. But it is the task of fundamental theology to detect the first signs of deep cultural shifts within Western thought, and of hitherto unaired questions which the new possibilities of dialogue with the great world religions address to a particular historical Christianity.

The specific occasion of this issue is provided by new forms of the questioning periodically directed against Christian monotheism.

Above all we have to acknowledge the increased liveliness of Judaism and Islam in this last quarter of the twentieth century. These transcendent religions are standing up admirably to the challenge of modern atheism and the growing success of immanentist religions originating in the East. But the gulf between their strict monotheism and the Trinitarian monotheism of Christianity tends to grow deeper. After moving beyond an often sterile and centuries-fold form of polemics, it is the historical task of Christians to prove in practice as in theory that the basic dogmas of the Incarnation and the Trinity do not compromise the divine oneness in any way.

Denunciation of the effects of monotheism on human societies is not a wholly contemporary phenomenon. Nevertheless to attack monotheism is once again fashionable in the Western cultural sphere. To paraphrase the title of Chateaubriand's famous *Génie du Christianisme*, some people talk freely of the 'genius of paganism'. Disillusioned by the bitter fruits of a triumphant secularisation, many contemporaries are looking for a new expression of the sacred dimension. They are trying to move beyond the alternatives of monotheism and atheism. In practice they are fighting on two fronts at one and the same time: against Marxism and Judaeo-Christianity. To a certain extent, this may be termed Nietzsche's revenge on Marx. The common error of Marxism and Christianity would be to defend a totalitarian notion of history, whereas paganism sees life, multiplicity, the maternal mystery of the earth, and the ever-new beginning of beauty and of the earth's activity—all these things—as sacred.

Some articles in this issue tackle this cultural phenomenon and ask whether it constitutes a pressing invitation to rediscover the original flavour of biblical monotheism; as it differs, that is, from the abstract unity of the God of theism.

Comparative history of religions has long called in question the *evolutionary* schema according to which the human religious consciousness is said to have passed successively through animist and polytheistic forms to arrive gradually at an increasingly refined form of monotheism. But a particular kind of Christian apologetics, which came into existence in the context of the great missionary era, sometimes still classifies the other world religions pejoratively as 'pagan'. It measures them by the yardstick of our own unique Judaeo-Christian monotheism conceived as 'absolute religion'.

One of the aims of this issue is to enable people to be more discerning in the use of convenient dualisms such as 'monotheism-polytheism', 'monism-pantheism', 'transcendence-immanence', and 'personal-impersonal'. After all, we must remember the formidable complexity of various religious systems. We are convinced, for instance, that better acquaintance with the major religions of the East, and a more vital awareness of the actual nature of Christianity, would caution us against a somewhat scornful view of polytheism, as if it were no more than an expression of some childhood ailment of the religious consciousness. Practice of a polytheistic religion does not absolutely exclude a highly elevated sense of a transcendent Absolute. Moreover, a counter-proof is the existence within Catholicism itself of many forms of popular religion (for example, the cult of the saints). These tend to compensate for the abstract universalism of a unique God who, for the very reason that he is everyone's, runs the risk of not being anyone's.

Finally a modern examination of monotheism cannot ignore the fact that, by using a monarchical and patriarchal image of God, it has served as an ideological guarantee for various forms of patriarchalism in and outside the West. The new feminist theologies are now questioning male power in family, State and Church, and are beginning to show its explicit or non-explicit links with a still patriarchal image of God. By proposing a new interpretation of Christian monotheism, not in a monarchical but in a truly Trinitarian sense, this issue of *Concilium* fulfils an undoubtedly theological task.

The articles summarised here are to be understood within this novel and varied context. We describe and discuss monotheism in three aspects. In the first part, comparative religion especially is called on to determine the specific nature of monotheism, and to assess the social and anthropological functions which are usually ascribed to it. The second part tries to restore the originality of biblical monotheism, and is a kind of prolegomenon to a theological investigation of Trinitarian monotheism as it differs above all from Islamic monotheism. A third section tries to look at some contemporary phenomena which bring monotheism more directly into question. Neo-paganism, the survival of the patriarchal system, the legitimate practice of popular religion, and the persistence of idol worship in the modern world are treated here. From a religious phenomenological viewpoint, E. Cornelis shows how deceptive the labels 'monotheism' and 'polytheism', 'monism' or 'pantheism' are when applied to the great world religions. Instead we must try to move beyond such alternatives as 'personal or impersonal', 'objectivity or subjectivity'. It is difficult, for instance, to define Indian monism in relation to various forms of theism, or to tie down the ultimate aim of Buddhism, by strict assignment to either transcendence or immanence as a category.

Periodic attempts are made to justify political absolutism on the basis of monotheism. In this regard many readers will be acquainted with E. Peterson's successful thesis on *Monotheism as a Political Problem*. Today, however, there is general agreement that this proposition has weak historical foundations. G. Ruggieri tries to pose in new terms the problem of connections between God and power. He suggests that neither the monotheistic religions, nor Trinitarian orthodoxy, lead of themselves to an ideological perversion of religion. This ideological degradation is observed instead when the religious imagination is deprived of its mystical horizon and is functionally reduced to an aspect of ethics.

Independently of its social and political function, however, we also have to ask whether monotheism has contributed to the development of the idea of the person. Attempts have even been made to assert that Judaeo-Christian monotheism, in contrast to the oriental religions, has been responsible for Western individualism. Against a broad historical background that includes ancient Greece, the mystery religions, traditional African religions and Judaeo-Christianity, M. Meslin studies the anthropocentric function of these various forms of monotheism. The human individual truly acquires the dignity of personhood not in creationist mythologies in which the transcendent God remains external to the world, but in the personal relationship with a God of Love and Providence inaugurated by Judaeo-Christian faith.

The second part of this issue, containing the theological contributions proper, starts with an article on biblical theology. Absolute monotheism is the gift to humanity of biblical religion. We asked B. Lang to retrace the major historical stages of the people of Israel's faith in the one God. It is not until Deutero-Isaiah and the Deuteronomic literature of the sixth and fifth centuries that we reach the culmination of a primitive monotheistic profession of faith which began some three hundred years earlier. But monotheism cannot be separated from the historical situation of the people of Israel. Their monotheism was a reaction to a crisis in which the God of the covenant was their only recourse. In short, soteriological monotheism is older than dogmatic monotheism.

J. Moltmann adopts a historical and dogmatic approach in his case for a soteriological monotheism. As against the Romanisation of the idea of God which culminated in the patriarchal monarchism of a 'Lord God', we have to return to the New Testament—especially to St John—and to depict the oneness of God in a Trinitarian and not a monotheistic aspect. Beyond *tritheism* and *modalism* the oneness of God is an open, attractive and inclusive unity. It is the only means of defeating the present criticisms of monotheism, which accuse it of serving to legitimate male power in family, State and Church.

In an especially thought-provoking article, Christian Duquoc sets out to undermine the thesis that monotheism was the origin of the Catholic Church's unitary ideology. History shows us that not all forms of monotheism are necessarily totalitarian and intolerant. Indeed, it may be said that it was much more the assumption by God of a particular history which led to intolerance. In practical terms, the hierarchicalised structure of the Church and its universalist practice gave monotheism this ideological function. In so doing, the Church contradicted the specific nature of Christian monotheism as a monotheism of the Trinitarian God—the point of which is precisely that it does not absolutise the unique nature of Jesus as the way to God.

B. Lang's study of biblical monotheism ends with the remark that it is more soteriological and dogmatic, and that consequently the religion of Israel sees hope as more radical than faith. The specific characteristic of Islamic monotheism, however, would seem to be its *dogmatism*. That, at least, is the opinion of R. Caspar, who examines the lasting significance of the monotheism of Islam. It is interesting in this regard that the problem of God's existence should be tackled only obliquely, through the problem of unicity. It is relatively easy to criticize Islam adversely for its inability to recognise basic Christian dogmas. It is more difficult to take note of the challenge which the strict monotheism of Islam continues to pose to Christianity, which has to reconcile the absolute unicity of God with the mysteries of the Trinity and the Incarnation.

Among questions of the moment covered in the third part of this issue, we asked A. Dumas to examine the novel attractiveness of neo-paganism, especially in the French cultural context. This trend is associated with the political movement known as the 'New Right'. In a return to paganism it seeks a third way beyond atheism and monotheism. Whereas the latter is said to encourage all forms of totalitarianism or egalitarianism, paganism, it is claimed, guarantees respect for differences between human beings and diverse expressions of life. Faced with the ambiguities of this form of sacralism, the best course would seem to be a demonstration of the advantages of biblical monotheism. For the monotheism of the Bible, a profession of faith in the one

God means the blessing of variety.

In a courageous article, J. Comblin defends popular religion in Latin America. He shows that in real life the cult of the saints acts as a corrective to the abstract universality of a God and a Jesus Christ who no longer enter into special relationships with human beings. Here, on this side of the gap between monotheism and polytheism, we may ask if there is not some strong link (in religious attitude, that is) between the 'pagan' religions of the peoples of Asia and Africa and the popular religion of traditional Christian nations. It is a matter of urgency to acknowledge that, just as the God of Israel could be both the God of the universe and the God of a particular people, so the Christian God is both the transcendent God and the liberating God of the poor and oppressed.

In the Bible the profession of strict monotheism always coincided with a condemnation of idols. We thought it would be opportune to conclude this number with an article on the status of contemporary idols. For this topic, G. Vahanian has produced a very personal reflection on the nature of language and the status of modern technology. He shows in particular that idolatry is no monopoly of polytheism or atheism. It fits monotheism just as well. The actual critique of idols begins with a critique of religious language, because it is language itself which is proof against idols. The return of the sacred is only a myth. The really disturbing thing is Christianity's bad conscience about technology, whereas the latter should itself be treated as an indirect result of the utopian iconoclasm of faith.

In offering this new issue to the readers of *Concilium*, we repeat our intention in this fundamental theology number to read the 'signs of the times'. The present critique of monotheism is one of those signs.

We shall have reached our goal if, in spite of the challenge of neo-paganism and the great non-monotheistic religions, this collection of articles helps us to rediscover the originality and attraction of Trinitarian monotheism.

CLAUDE GEFFRÉ
JEAN-PIERRE JOSSUA

Translated by J. G. Cumming

PART I

Historical Perspectives

Etienne Cornélis

The Imprecise Boundaries of Notions of the Ultimate

1. LABELS ARE DECEPTIVE

WAYS OF conceiving a personal Supreme Being, an impersonal first and final principle of all things, or various gods, ways of denying their existence or any possible connection between them and the course of cosmic or human affairs—all this does not come from nowhere. Without going so far as to consider them as the stages of a necessary historical itinerary, of which the laws could be discovered, it must nevertheless be recognised that there are too many convergent pointers, which all tend to indicate a quite close relationship between the historical destiny of human societies and the theological theories which they produce, for us not to consider them most seriously when we attempt to think out afresh the meaning of the labels currently applied in this context. No pure concept, elaborated in the abstract, is perfectly adequate, here even less than in other spheres, to lived experience.

We should not be discouraged by this observation, for, after all, a revision of the labels proves to be one of the best ways of seeking to perceive in what way recent historical developments might influence the very way of posing the problem. An article such as this is forced to proceed elliptically. To arrogate this right to oneself is equivalent to supposing the results of a great quantity of patient historical analyses to be known and generally accepted. They provide the basis for any classification into types. To bring together and verify the totality of the historical knowledge which is necessary is beyond the capability of anyone, in particular the author of this article; having specialised above all in Indian philosophy and religion, having some knowledge of Christian

3

theology and the philosophy of religion, but having only a superficial knowledge of Islamic theology and philosophy, I have chosen to follow a course which is in accordance with this lacuna. Considering that the theologies and philosophies which have emerged from monotheistic cultures principally define their conception of the divine Absolute by distinguishing it by contrast with that which their culture has rejected (and sometimes failed to appreciate), we shall begin from what they reject in order to examine to what extent this rejection leads them to elaborate a caricature of living reality and to exaggerate the differences in order not to have to consider in depth certain problems arising from the heart of their own history.

We have therefore chosen to listen first to those whom we label pejoratively (whereas they name themselves with pride) monists or pantheists. The complexity of the beliefs of those whom we describe with too vague approximation as polytheists is such that it would be impossible to do them justice in a few pages.

2. THE DIVIDING LINE BETWEEN EASTERN ARYANS

This listening to other faiths is obviously dependent on the historical documentation at our disposal. We must also choose the crossroads of history at which we shall listen. There is one which seemed good to take as a starting point. The tribes speaking the Indo-European tongue who, in their great migration, took the most eastward route divided into one group which traversed the Khyber Pass in about 1500 BC and another which established itself on the Iranian plateau. The former left us the Vedas, the latter the Avesta. It is true that these texts reveal an obvious polytheism, sometimes closely connected in nature and structure, and nearly always comparable, to that of the Greeks, Romans, Teutons and Slavs, but a polytheism in the process of transformation into a more unified vision of the divine. At the heart of the Avesta are found the famous Gāthā of which the author was more than probably Zarathustra himself, the prophet of Ahura Mazda; at the end of the Veda (Skr: *vedānta*) are found the ancient Aranyakas and Upanishads, destined to become the most influential part of the inspired texts on which Hinduism is founded.

If Zoroaster was a reformer who rejected part of the tradition, remodelled that part which he did adopt and finally stamped his powerful work with a personal monotheistic emphasis (which was to be partially effaced through the effect of polytheistic inertia and dualistic complaisance) the *Brihadāranyaka Upanishad* brings us, for its part, the fruit of the daring meditations of a Brahmin named Yājñavalkya, who as a religious personality was in no way inferior to Zoroaster himself and who formulated the aphorisms which were destined to nourish and legitimise the monistic religiosity of the entire Vedantic tradition.

Zarathustra and Yājñavalkya both departed resolutely from the beaten track of polytheism. Zarathustra with an undisguised aggressiveness, reminiscent of the prophetic anger of the Bible and the Koran, Yājñavalkya with a philosophical serenity free from any scorn, but, if not as explicitly, quite as radically demythologising as was to be that of the Buddha, three or four centuries later. To speak of monotheism where Zarathustra is concerned is not current practice nowadays. The label currently used in this context is dualist. In fact, Zarathustra's doctrine is neither more nor less dualistic than that of certain Qum'ran writings and its ultimate intention is no less monotheistic than theirs. If there is a dualism in Zarathustra's doctrine, it is a dualism of the deuteronomic type, and therefore essentially ethical. It sets before each believer a moral choice with practical consequences, a choice which will determine his ultimate destiny. In the case of Yājñavalkya it is not a question of a moral choice of this kind, but rather of an esoteric wisdom, of a saving 'Know thyself'.

This divergence between two soteriological doctrines becomes even more meaningful if it is accepted, as is more than probable, than the previous traditions, common to the Aryans of India and those of Iran, normally sought salvation in the scrupulous performance of a sacrificial rite in which gods and men shared table fellowship, repeating an original and originating mythical rite through which both the cosmic order and the social order had been established.

Mazdaism was born of the rejection of the demoniac practices of polytheism, but was to remain centred on a fire cult. Vedantic Hinduism was to tolerate all rites and honour all gods, whilst feeling free to reinterpret them, but would insist on the meditative approach to the mystery of the One without a second, impersonal, ultimately situated beyond good and evil.

3. THE SAME JUSTICE FOR ALL

Did Zoroaster have some knowledge of the Israelite prophetic tradition? No solid proof of this can be provided and the chances of it are extremely slim.[1] Moreover, his God, Ahura Mazda, the Wise Lord who sees everything, has a homologue who is highly placed in the most ancient Vedic pantheon, Varuna, in whose person the Vedas have preserved for us the most important features of the Indo-Iranian divinity chosen by Zoroaster to occupy, alone, the zenith of his heaven. Just as Ahura Mazda is particularly associated with Asha, or Justice, it is Varuna's responsibility to maintain order (*rita*, etymologically identical to Asha) in the universe. Having eyes everywhere is, moreover, an attribute which is common to the two divinities. If the social implications of the Zoroastrian reform are self-evident, it is nonethelesss true that his monotheism allows to survive within it, implicitly, the earlier polytheistic structures, which allow him to account more easily for the existence in nature and society of divergent forces, which are at times mutually opposed and which resist attempts to reduce them to a unitary concept. Similar motives led Hindu monism to make room for a doctrine of retribution for human actions (the law of *karma*) intended to explain and legitimise the existence of castes. On such points the Yahwistic prophetic tradition proves to be more intransigent in its bias towards the widow, the orphan and even the foreigner.

The historical reasons which led Zarathustra to opt for a militant monotheism, allied to a quasi-ontological moral dualism, at the time when Yājñavalkya was choosing the way of monism allied to an ascesis of the yogic type and a mystical theology of respect for all life, will, doubtless, never become entirely clear. It remains for us to examine whether these contrasting historical twins can provide religious typology with two models of universal validity.

According to one present-day view, an authentic spiritualistic monism originates from the objectification, immanent within the consciousness, of the Subject considered as a representation, and consequently denies the autonomous reality of matter. Now if it is true that the doctrine of the *Ātman* or absolute Self is at the basis of Advaitist monism, it is by no means certain, and even probably untrue, that the notion of the *Ātman* is merely the product of the objectification of the self-representation formed by the Subject. In fact, this representation has a name in Indian speculative philosophy: the *āhamkāra* (that which makes the 'I') and Brahmin philosophers rapidly came to see in it the major obstacle to the achievement of salvation. On the other hand, the realisation of the *Ātman* is identical with the ultimate goal. Such a realisation implies passing definitively beyond the duality of subject and object.[2] That which is merely superficial appearance, *māyā*, is the multiplicity of the material furnished by the senses, and our individuality localised in space and time. (It is not, moreover, without some justification that modern Hindu philosophers have recognised in the thought of Bradley the Western philosophy of which the ideas seemed most closely related to their own). Indian monism has, however, had variants which were more vitalistic and pantheistic than the *advaita* of Śaṃkara, variants in which since the entire universe is merely a *macranthropos*, the natural elements, fire, water, air, correspond to the three humours, bile, serosities, breath, whose interaction gives life to all living beings.

If we attempt to define Indian monism in relation to the different forms which may be assumed by theism, the difficulty will lie in coming to an agreement on what constitutes a 'person'. The spontaneous response of the Judeo-Christian and Roman tradition is to see this as a moral person, which coincides which the most important insight of Zoroastrianism. Now, if the monism of Śaṃkara gives, in spiritual practices, a major place to an Iśvara, a Lord with personal attributes, capable of concentrating the attention of the devotee and inspiring his adoration, this Iśvara does not, however, appear as a Judge and hardly as a Creator (he is rather the first being having emanated from the impersonal absolute principle to be individualised). In fact, Iśvara is only a 'god-from-our-point-of-view', corresponding to the limited mode of knowledge of which beings are capable whilst they have not yet overcome in the *samādhi* the opposition of subject and object. The Śaṃkaran form of monism is complicated by a dualistic epistemology which distinguishes between two notions of truth, one which is valid absolutely and the other which is valid in so far as subject and object still remain opposed.

4. MORAL REQUIREMENTS AND METAPHYSICAL REQUIREMENTS

Solutions of this kind, intended to resolve similar logical difficulties, are found wherever tranquil belief (the faith of the charcoal burner) has given place to controversy and speculation and men have recourse to logical artifice to put an end to debate. It has even been suggested that recourse to speculation has the effect, in practice and in the long term, of depriving the religious impulse of its original energy. In reality the real paradox lies elsewhere. The most powerfully religious minds are often also those which demand a high level of morality and logicality, both from themselves and from others. Where the moral requirement is dominant, the purification of religion tends towards monotheism, for it is interpersonal relations, justice, love and their opposites which occupy the foreground and this, moreover, leads logically to the more or less overt introduction of dualism, in one form or another. Where the logico-metaphysical requirement of unity becomes dominant, everything, including logic itself, finally becomes involved. The full monism of Parmenides will itself be overtaken on this path by the empty monism of a Nāgārjuna, whereas the *māyā*, the advaitist cosmic illusion, is merely a shameful subterfuge which is obliged to admit its logical flimsiness through the elaboration of a theory of two levels of truth, i.e. of a gnoseological dualism. The question therefore arises as to whether it is first of all the demands of a gnoseological and gnostical logic which send religious minds into mystical orbit, or whether, on the contrary, it is an experience of oceanic consciousness of the *samādhi* type which leaves them no alternative but to reduce to the disruptive absurdity of a *koan* the fundamental laws of our common human thought.

The monotheist prophet does not suffer from such metaphysical or mystical obsessions. And yet, if he believes that his God of justice is also the creator, which is generally the case, he is unavoidably confronted by similar difficulties even though they are situated in another register, that of the questionings of a Job or a Qohelet about the origins and the meaning of a world in which evil is so obviously at home. The recourse to one variant or another of 'original sin' must lead to a breach in the unitary system of his personalist monotheism. In the end the theologian, like St Lawrence on his gridiron, will always be roasted, whether by the mystical right or the prophetic left. Renouvier, who characterises the God of the mystics as the 'Absolute' God and that of the prophets as the 'Moral Person' God, declares them to be logically incompatible.[3] Perhaps he has not seen that the logic of the mystic is a metalogic which, starting from the experience of the *unio mystica*, uses logic to demolish the pretentions of logic to impose conditions on the Absolute. Mystical theology teaches its followers to traverse interminably the *via negativa*, which the prophets do not do, not only because they are too preoccupied elsewhere but particularly because they cannot risk undermining the causal link between the fault and the punishment, a logical relation which they need in order to constrain the wayward to return to the path of righteousness. If India has been able to devote itself, without this 'prophetic' restriction, to mystical speculation and trans-ethical ecstasies it is because, in Indian thought, the logic of action had been entrusted, once and for all, to a cosmic mechanism, the law of *karma*, thus dispensing with the necessity for the personal intervention of a just and omniscient Judge. There remained the task of understanding the relationship between a practically autonomous universe, the place of karmic retribution, and the existence of a superior principle, personal or impersonal, of which the free existence in itself, once revealed or experienced, must by definition break the circular process, without beginning or end, of causes and effects.

5. PASSING BEYOND UNDERSTANDING

If it is relatively easy, in the name of a certain kind of logic, to reject equally the prophets' God-Judge and the mystics' impersonal Absolute, it is, on the other hand, far too easy to reject the divine of the mystics as a product of mere subjectivity (possibly dazzled—that is its excuse—by the experience of oceanic consciousness), whereas the God of the prophets, on the contrary, would alone enjoy the guarantee of objectivity, since he reveals himself from the outside to his creature, who would be quite incapable on his own of conceiving him 'for himself'. It is no more true to limit to mere subjectivity the meaning of mystical experience than it is to see only objectivity in the prophetic act of receiving a revelation. A Nāgārjuna, for example, a Buddhist theologian and therefore in the mystical tradition, is perfectly conscious of the snares of subjectivity when he shows that the method and the ultimate goal of Buddhism cannot be contained either in the category of transcendance nor in that of immanence, or, in the terms of his own vocabulary, are not classifiable either under the term *nirvāṇa* or the term *samsāra*. Implicitly, this means rejecting, in absolute truth, all dilemmas such as those involving 'personal' or 'impersonal', 'object' or 'subject', 'objectivity' or 'subjectivity'. Nāgārjuna's position implies also that there is no eternal substantial entity and 'first cause'. The notion of the transcendental void (*shūnyatā*) which appears as the keystone of the other negations of the *via negativa* is itself subject to its own effectiveness in emptying concepts of all meaning and cannot therefore stand in place of such an entity. One must no doubt go even further and recognise that the mystical experience designated by the term *bodhi*, in which is 'revealed' (to whom ?) the insubstantial nature of all phenomena, itself falls beneath the logical scalpel of this all-dissolving analysis for the same reason as do all other 'names-and-forms' (*nāmarūpa*).

It should moreover, be evident from first principles that the quality of experience which may be demanded of a 'real' prophet not only surpasses his little self but must also surpass his understanding, in a way which is entirely analogous to the effect produced by mystical experience, so as to have the moral right to compel the prophet's unconditional belief and to give him the right to carry by storm the adhesion of others! The fact that mystics do not always emerge from this experience with a message to transmit (unlike the prophet-mystics Zarathustra, Isaiah, Gautama, Jesus, Mohammed or Al-Hallāj) certainly raises a problem. This difficulty can be resolved if one admits that the full moral implications of certain authentic mystical experiences are not always perceived. The man who has just enjoyed a transpersonal beatific state has a duty to invite all who are still prisoners of the finiteness of their self to experience the same self-transcendence as he has known.

In addition, the authentically prophetic quality emanating from certain mystical figures must be recognised, even when, through fidelity to their experience in the heart of the cloud of unknowing, they believe that they must not attribute any personal characteristics to their absolute. Again, on this point one must keep in mind the possibility that their denial of the personal character of their absolute may stem from an over-narrow concept of 'person' which deprives it of a possible analogical extension in the transpersonal sense.

What must be recognised in any hypothesis is the fact that there is a mystical mode of projecting a god or an impersonal absolute (e.g. Brahman) which encompasses cosmic totality, sometimes conceived of as 'his' body, and that this perception of the absolute does not coincide with that testified to by the prophets. Their experience obliges them to enlist on the side of God at the heart of the conflicts which are inherent to the human condition throughout history.

6. EXPERIENCE AND SPECULATION

One of the most important, but also most difficult aspects of the phenomenological definition of monotheism within the general area of representation of the divine concerns the distinction between the contribution of experience and that of speculation to the forms taken by traditional beliefs. First, one cannot exclude the possibility that a representation of the divine formulated as the result of a religious experience may refer, *a priori*, to something other than a representation resulting from a process of reasoning (which might, after all, be only a sophism). It is also possible that a representation of the divine, born of an experience, is then filtered through a process of reasoning and controversy from which it emerges with its individuality smoothed away. Conversely, the problematic which has already been elaborated within a particular religious culture around the theme of the divine or the ultimate inevitably imposes on the expression of even the most original religious experience the interplay of its traditional alternatives. Finally, the philosopher who is most critical of the basic premisses of religion, in other people as well as himself, remains potentially, whether he wishes it or not, an existentially religious man, a fact which cannot fail to affect his speculation as soon as it approaches those uncertain areas into which his reason leads him at the risk of unverifiability.

It is thus that the India of the classical period, having reached the stage at which logical thought, having become self-consciously aware of its methodological requirements, encouraged the upsurge of scholastic controversies between the different schools of religious thought, nevertheless never attempted to establish clear boundaries between philosophy and theological speculation.

Was it mere chance that it was precisely in India that the quest for mystical union displayed at the same time the greatest daring and the most rigorous method? And would this not explain the fact that, seen from the viewpoint of a

Western world trained in the school of Greek thought, Indian religious thought appears as totally originating from and dependent on a mystical experience which favours, on principle, procedures of an apophatic nature developing from the 'neti neti'[4] (non-da, non-da) of the Brihadāraṇyaka Upanishad? This Indian thought almost never loses sight of the fact that the very nature of religious experience makes difficult, and even rebels against, the exercise of a certain kind of rational control—a realisation which in no way corresponds to an attitude of irrationalism, but, on the contrary, is allied to insistence on a high standard of rationality. The power and the rigorousness of Indian speculative reasoning are in no way inferior to what the West has attained in this sphere.

It is therefore somewhat risky to pretend to distinguish, in the phemomenology of religion, what elements result from experience and what results from speculation. This does not make the attempt valueless, for it is only in this way that it will be possible to indicate which expressions, logically incompatible, might nevertheless refer to experiences which are identical, or at least not mutually exclusive. Royce, in his article in Hastings's Encyclopedia, has already made this point with regard to the essential distinction between monotheism, pantheism and monism. Logically, the proposition 'God is One' does not exclude the possibility of this God's being identical with the whole of reality, and a certain conception of God should, indeed, lead to this as a necessary consequence. Therefore the second experience (God is All) can only be considered to contradict the first (God is One) either because of differences of experience which go beyond mere logic, or because of different conceptions of God.

According to one's definition of 'god', there may be several gods or there may only be one, or there may only be one and nothing outside him. Or again, the proposition 'God is a Person' may or may not exclude the proposition 'God alone exists', either because of the specific nature of the religious experience, or because of different definitions of the concept of 'person'. The ascription of any attribute whatever to God, once he has been located on the level of the absolute, necessitates in addition the elevation of that attribute to a degree of supereminence which compromises its unequivocal meaning. The accumulation of aporiae around the single point in the field of discourse which is the (pseudo?)-concept of God renders any change of position extremely dangerous. At the pole, the compass goes berserk. The refusal, for example, to recognise in the objects of empirical experience the same reality as one attributes to God may result from two different sources of judgment. If for Eckhart or Śaṃkara, without wishing to deny the part played by the demands of logic and metaphysics, it seems to be religious experience which has the decisive influence in carrying conviction, for Spinoza, without wishing to exclude the part played, in the insistence on rigorousness of his philosophical consciousness, by the monotheistic tradition of Judaism, it seems very probable that it is the metaphysical requirement which is more significant that the religious experience. The use of the same word, 'monism', in these three cases will therefore lead to confusion.

The double action, both religious and logical, of experience as well as theoretical discourse, is shown in exemplary fashion in the history of the Vedanta, by the distinctions which Rāmānuja was anxious to emphasise by contrast with Śaṃkara. These theoretical distinctions are undoubtedly due to an incompatibility in their respective religious experiences, with Rāmānuja refusing to sacrifice in favour of the non-dualism, *apparently* more logical and less religious, of Śaṃkara, the concept of the persistence of a beatific relationship at the heart of the ultimate state. If Rāmānuja intends, nevertheless, to remain faithful to the traditional postulates of the Vedanta, it is for reasons which do not belong to pure logic, pure metaphysics or pure fidelity to a religious tradition. A student of the *Bhagavad-Gītā*, Rāmānuja respects its apparent inconsequentialities as the expression, necessarily ambiguous, of an absolute which is neither personal nor impersonal. Although transcending the logic proper to finite persons, such an absolute cannot in any way lack anything of what the experience which a person has of himself and of his interpersonal relationships would suggest in the way of beatific plenitude. In that sense the a-problematical inconsequentialities of the Gītā,[5] which became, following the reductionist advaitist exigesis of Śaṃkara, problematical in Rāmānuja, are analogous to the polytheistic inconsequentialities of the Gospels, which became problematical during and after the first ecumenical councils.

If this comparison is at all enlightening, it may also help us to situate in a single phenomenological area both the absolute Brahman of Śaṃkara and the monolithic only God of the profession of faith of Islam, by way of the one- and threefold God of Christian theology.

7. INCOMPATIBLE EXPRESSIONS OF COMPATIBLE EXPERIENCES

If Śaṃkara, in his commentary on the Gītā, places the text on the Procrustean bed of his non-dualism, it is not primarily because of his logical fidelity to a theological postulate, but because of a fervour, which is no doubt equivalent to that of Rāmānuja, but originating from a different religious experience. If Nicaea is quite unacceptable to a disciple of Mohammed, if each great Council left behind a trail of 'heresies', it is not only because of different theoretical approaches to the same problem, nor even because of differing religio-political interests, but at least as much, if not more, because of experiences which had been lived differently and were therefore differently structured. If two contradictory theories cannot both be true simultaneously, this is not the case with two different religious experiences, even if their classical expression makes them appear to be incompatible. The religious experience of divine justice, for example, in no way excludes the religious experience of divine freewill. The 'Pelagian' affirmation of ancient Buddhism, that we shall only attain salvation by our own efforts, emerged from a religious experience which was in no way incompatible with that, apparently quietist in its expression, of an Amidist Buddhist declaring that the only attitude which brings salvation is to rely on grace alone.

It is because he made the *religious* discovery of the necessity of considering as simultaneously true and false the most diametrically opposed affirmations that Nāgārjuna became, in all the sects of the Buddhism of the Great Vehicle, a patriarch practically equal in authority to Gautama. In short, if the excellent thinker Nāgārjuna strove to dismantle the principles and laws of logical thought until he made them into puppets without strings, it was not for the masochistic pleasure of driving himself and others mad, but to bring the healing remedies of religion to the place where there is a danger that the disease will be hardest to detect, that is, in the good conscience which results from the correctness of logical reasoning (which does not mean that he would deny the Gospel precept, 'Let your yes be yes and your no, no'!).

The follower of the Judeo-Christian religious tradition prefers spontaneously, if not necessarily, certain expressions, which have become classic, of certain religious experiences, those narrated by the Canon and transmitted by the Tradition. Among these, there are two or three which occupy a particularly privileged place, that of Abraham, that of Moses and that of Jesus. They only come to us, however, through the same intermediary of the texts and their traditional interpretation as do the others. In the case of Jesus, for example, there is a sufficient consensus around the authenticity of the name 'Abba', as a privileged expression of his personal relationship to the divine, for us to attempt to characterise by this the particular flavour of the monotheism which such an expression supposes. Since this question will certainly be discussed elsewhere in this issue of the journal, I shall not dwell on it except from my own viewpoint, to situate this particular case within the sphere of those experiences of the divine attested by history and able to be compared with each other by religious phenomenology.

A short, but steep road to attain this goal begins from the unique confrontation with monotheist faith to be found in the Pali canon: 'Those who attribute everything to the creation of a Lord have lost all taste for action, no longer make any effort to do this thing and avoid that'.[6] It is therefore in the name of the upholding of morality and of a possibility of working for one's own salvation that the existence of an almighty God is questioned here. And yet Buddhists are not ignorant of the fact that a transcendance beyond phenomena is a necessary datum to motivate man's effort towards supreme good: 'There is a not-born, not-becoming, not-created, not-conditioned; if there were not, there would be no way out'.[7] What they reject is the moral laxity which they see as the inevitable consequence of the attitude of confident abandon of the devotees of creationist monotheism.

It is nevertheless clear that the monotheist faith which takes as its model the filial relationship of Jesus to his 'Abba' is not liable to such criticism.

A Father who wants nothing to do with mercenaries, but seeks on the contrary to adopt sons in order to make them collaborators with him in a wild enterprise of liberation through the sheer love of pure friendship, has nothing in common with the sort of god seeking passive worshippers who is rejected by Buddhism.

It is true on the other hand that, under the banner of monotheism, many forms of fanaticism have assembled in the past and still gather their cohorts today to exterminate the 'infidel'. There are, however, other ways of averting this threat than atheism. Yes, with its empty monism (*Shūnyatā*) and the mercifulness of its Bodhisattvas, the Mahāyāna is certainly one way; following in the steps of a Son, who, in loving obedience, gives up his lordly prerogatives to share the lot of the hopeless and thus gives them back a wild hope, is another way. Why should the absolute hiding beyond the horizon of these two convergent ways of merciful generosity not be, despite the labels, in practice one?

Translated by L. H. Ginn

Notes

1. R. Mayer's definitive study 'Monotheismus in Israel und in der Religion Zarathustras' *Bibl. Zsch* (n.f.1, 1957) 23–58, does not seem to me ever to have been refuted on this point.

2. Here, in Senart's translation, is a convincing passage from the *Brihadāraṇyaka Upanishad* 4,3: 31–33: 'Although the Ātman does not know, he nevertheless remains capable of knowing; knowledge does not escape the knower that he is, for it is indestructible; only, there is no second, no other and separate object, which he can know. It is only when another object exists that one can see that other (. . .). In the middle of the ocean, a single perceiver, without a second object to perceive, such is, o king, the world of *Brahman*, thus taught Yājñavalkya. There is the supreme goal, the supreme achievement, the supreme world, the supreme felicity.'

3. C. Renouvier *Traité de logique* (1864) t. II p. 355.
4. *Brihadāranyaka Up.* 4, 2 : 4.
5. G. Parrinder *Avatar and Incarnation* (London 1970) p. 119.
6. *Anguttara* I : 174.
7. *Itivuttaka* 43.

Giuseppe Ruggieri

God and Power: A Political Function of Monotheism?

1. THE HISTORICAL BACKGROUND

CRITICISM OF religion because of its links with temporal power is widespread in the modern world. The Enlightenment, socialism and Marxism have all developed their own versions of this criticism. What is perhaps less well known is that there is an original variant of this questioning within Christian theology: a probing of whether monotheist religions are responsible for the alliance between belief in God and political power, whereas the orthodox Christian conception of a triune God renders religious justification of any particular political order impossible. This process began within early nineteenth century German Catholicism, with a reading of the history of Arianism as it affected ecclesial politics. J. A. Möhler, in the 1827, first, edition of his book on Athanasius, had already affirmed that the Arians' faith in the Saviour as a limited being lowered the idea of a universal Church to that of a mere State Church. In January 1838, the first edition of Joseph Görres's *Athanasius* appeared, in which the subsequently exiled Bishop of Alexandria appeared not merely as the defender of the divinity of the Son of God, but above all as the model of a politics aimed at securing the freedom of the Church from the State and its absolutist pretensions. Görres wrote his book in the space of a few weeks, following the imprisonment of the Archbishop of Cologne, Clemens August von Droste zu Vischering, accused of opposition to the measures of the Prussian government regarding mixed marriages. The book had an immense success and was largely responsible for the fact that anti-Arian trinitarian orthodoxy is often seen as having political as well as theological overtones.

The most eminent representative of this historical current in this century has been Erik Peterson (1890–1960). A lecturer in the evangelical theology faculty of the University of Bonn, he became a Catholic at the end of 1930. A determined opponent of Nazism, he published an essay in Leipzig in 1935 bringing together two earlier studies, on the subject of *'monarchia divina'* and the verdict of early Christianity on the Emperor Augustus. The essay was entitled *Der Monotheismus als politisches Problem* and in it Peterson began, in the Foreword, by denouncing the European Enlightenment for its reduction of the fullness of Christian belief in God to mere monotheism. This reduction he saw as a lethal tendency leading to existentialism, whereas political monotheism was something alien to original Christianity, being rather elaborated, within the development of Christianity, by the apologists who adopted the framework of Judaic religious propaganda worked out by Philo. The monotheistic thesis was a useful defence for Christians accused of being enemies of the State. It was Origen's disciple, the 'court theologian' Eusebius, who linked monotheism with justification of the Roman Empire, by interpreting the *pax augustea* as a willed effect of divine providence in order to prepare the way for the diffusion of the Christian Gospel among newly subject peoples. The traditional argument of Greek political theology, according to which a single God set above everything served as a basis for expressing and justifying the unique dignity of the earthly sovereign, was thereby adapted by Eusebius to the historical theology of the Christian event. The main arguments by which Eusebius developed his particular vision were these:

(*a*) The end of separate nation States and their incorporation into the one Roman Empire was due to divine providence. This unification in fact favoured the proclamation of the good news since this was no longer hampered by the existence of national frontiers.

(*b*) The plurality of autonomous States brought with it the risk of wars, whereas the Roman Empire brought about the eschatological peace promised by the prophets.

(*c*) To the one ruler on earth corresponded the one God, only ruler of the heavens above.

(*d*) A pluralist world produces a polytheist metaphysic. With the ending of nation States, polytheism itself lost the right to exist.

According to Peterson, it was this link between divine kingship and the Roman Empire that prevented Eusebius from expressing orthodox trinitarian doctrine. Once the orthodox dogma of the Trinity had been formulated, on the other hand, the Christian concept of 'divine kingship' lost its theological-political character. This development, still according to Peterson, was brought about by the Cappadocian Fathers; thanks to orthodox dogma, 'not only was monotheism theologically done away with as a political problem and

Christian faith freed from its imprisonment in the Roman Empire, but more fundamentally, a break was achieved from each and every "political theology", which degrades the Christian message into justification of a political situation. Anything like a "political theology" can only exist on the level of Judaism or paganism.'

In this essay, Peterson was crossing swords with Carl Schmitt, who in his 1922 publication *Politische Theologie: Vier Kapitel zur Lehre von der Souveranität*, had upheld the link between the political ordering of society and metaphysical and theological ideas, even in the secularising orders typical of the modern age. But in the years immediately following its publication, Peterson's essay made no notable mark on theological discussion properly so called. This was left to J. B. Metz, who in his *Zur Theologie der Welt* of 1968 somewhat casually took up Peterson's thesis, even becoming protagonist of a 'political theology', though a 'new' one. Metz, however, did not develop the trinitarian argument, preferring the 'eschatological reserve' as the characteristic of the believer who refuses any identification between the Christian message and the claims of any historical political subject. It was left to Jürgen Moltmann to develop the relationship between trinitarian theology and criticism of political power. Among critics of Peterson, one should perhaps single out Carl Schmitt himself, who in 1970 published *Politische Theologie II*, with the suggestive subtitle, 'The myth of the demise of all political theology'. Besides him, K. Hungar and A. Schindler have devoted a concentrated period of research to Peterson's thesis; this took place at Heidelberg and its conclusions were published in *Monotheismus als politisches Problem? Erik Peterson und die Kritik der politischen Theologie* ed. A. Schindler (Gütersloh, 1978). Their conclusions are devastating: of Peterson's historical argument, hardly one stone remains on another.

2. A NEW STATEMENT OF THE QUESTION

The question raised by Peterson is both vague and fascinating at the same time. It needs to be re-stated if the truth of his position is not to be lost. To this end, some brief observations may be made, even though there is not space to develop them fully on this occasion.

(*a*) Not only monotheism, but trinitarian belief too has *in fact* been linked to a political theology used to justify the existing political order. Eusebius himself justified the fact that Constantine had three successors as an imitation of the Trinity. Theologians who held orthodox trinitarian views were also 'political theologians' in the sense intended by Peterson, and even 'court theologians'. Following the orthodox definition of the dogma of the Trinity, the links between the Church and the Roman Empire did not come to an end, particularly in the East. And the history of the Byzantine Empire includes the famous acclamation of Heraclius and Tiberius as co-rulers with Constantine IV Pogonatus: 'We believe in the Trinity; we here crown the three'.

(b) Monotheism too has in fact known relationships with the prevailing power that were not justificatory but critical. Two examples can stand here for a wealth of others, one drawn from contemporary Hebrahism and one from medieval Islam.

Louis Massignon has shown the West the enormous richness of the mystical and religious traditions of Islam, including the legacy of Hallâj.[1] His religious thought and practice belong to a great monotheistic tradition and show a relationship to authority which is not, precisely from religious conviction, that of a theology serving politics, but one rich in mystical and martyrological overtones. Hallâj (857–922) was a counsellor to princes against his wishes, and quite the opposite of a court theologian; he was put to death by the authorities not through any fateful turn of events, but as a result of his own inner choice and convictions.

The second example is that of Martin Buber, always ready to deny the political adaptation of biblical theocracy adopted by several currents of contemporary political Zionism. A few sentences from his Königtum Gottes (Heidelberg, 1956) can serve to illustrate his position: 'The positive content of the covenant on Sinai consists in showing that the wandering tribes adopted JHWH as their king "for time and for eternity"; its negative side consists in showing that on the other hand no man can call himself king of the sons of Israel . . . JHWH does not wish to be, like many a monarchical divinity, sovereign and guarantor of a human monarchy; the man to whom he sometimes entrusts the enactment of his will not only possesses power only within this context, but cannot in turn transfer any power to beyond this limited extent . . .' (p. 115).

(c) Also, it is not easy to grasp the exact meaning of Peterson's essay. I have said that it was based on two earlier studies; these were: 'Göttliche Monarchie', which appeared in Theologische Quartalschrift in 1931, and 'Kaiser Augustus im Urteil des antiken Christentums . . .', published in Hochland in 1932/3. The original intention behind these two essays was not identical. The one on 'divine kingship' referred mainly to the theme of the Trinity and documented the reception of the idea of the kingship of God in pre-Cappadocian Christian theology. In this study the connection between political theology and trinitarian doctrine has not yet become a motive of critical reflection. The explicit reference to the 'political theology' of Carl Schmitt is, however, present in the study of the early Christian judgment of Augustus. And in fact, if one reads the essay on monotheism carefully, the true force of Peterson's argument, that which can reasonably be said to demonstrate an effective connection between acquiescence in the political situation and the teaching of Eusebius, does not lie in the field of trinitarian doctrine but in that of eschatology. The process by which Eusebius utilises the concept of divine kingship to attribute a privileged role in Christian economy to Constantine becomes secondary to the process of 'de-eschatologisation' in Eusebius' thought: that the prophetic promise is realised in the peace brought about by the empire.

Furthermore, the strength of Peterson's argument is linked to another aspect, which is typical of his theological thought in the strict sense, not tied to historical analysis. Peterson was influenced by pietism, and in the years prior to his conversion to Catholicism he was already looking for a way out from the 'liberal' reduction of Christianity (represented for him by Harnack above all) other than that traced by the dialectical theology of Karl Barth. He thought he had found this way out in *dogma* as such. Dogma, with its authoritative claim, continues the Incarnation and represents the specific actions by which God pursues man through history. But Peterson did not understand dogma in an objectivist sense, as the abstract content of a faith, but rather in its links with faith. For Peterson it was the confession of faith that made up the substance of martyrdom, of that witness to the truth that the Church must give to the world, while always maintaining the eschatological difference between this truth and any commitment, any historical situation.[2] So, in other words, it would seem that the deep meaning of Peterson's thesis is to be found not in a simplistic remit to the pure 'content' of trinitarian faith, like a safeguard against any possible ideological utilisation of Christianity, but in the intuition that makes up the *orthodox profession* of faith, which implies adoration and the obedience owed to the truth of the God of Jesus Christ, the only possible way in which truth can escape from *possession* by an earthly authority.

(*d*) What exactly do we mean by monotheism? S. Breton has recently posed the problem with great insight, writing as a philosopher, but in such a way as to pose a deep challenge to theologians, in his *Unicité et monothéisme* (Paris, 1981). When we speak of one God in biblical and Christian tradition are we in fact trying to describe a constituent property of God or the uniqueness of a mediation, that of the chosen people first and then that of the crucified and risen Christ, a mediation which constitutes the only possible access to God? And does the uniqueness of this mediation not lie in the fact that it guarantees access to God to all peoples and every person, that it provides the pneumatological means by which a particular historical experience is opened out to accept the many?

Without trying to answer these questions, which would involve a decision on the actual meaning of human discourse about God, it is worth recalling that, particularly in the Eastern Christian tradition, stress has always been laid on the ultimate unknowability of the *ousia* of God, which means that it is only a conceptual representation that allows access to God. Neither 'the One' nor 'the Good' encapsulate or exhaust the ultimate depth of God. This understanding led Gregory Palamas to distinguish between divine essence and divine energy, on the grounds that the doctrine of trinitarian procession itself establishes a distance between our discourse about God and the mystery of God himself. The final meaning of this theological stance is that God is not an object or concept belonging to our world of thought, but an unfathomable mystery. The central problem of discourse on God is not that of making God known, but of purifying ourselves so that we can stand in his presence. This presence of God can be grasped only through a process of transcending, of *ekstasis* with regard to all our conceptual habits.

In the biblical tradition, the culminating point of this process by which human discourse *is* at the same time the presence of God is to be found in the Cross of Jesus of Nazareth. This brings together the full manifestation of the mystery and complete nakedness, radical emptiness and the absolute fulness of love on the part of him who gives himself. But this implies that the uniqueness of the mystery here revealed cannot be assimilated to any concept that can be made functional or organic to any particular representation of the world.

3. MYSTICISM AND ETHICS

The preceding observations lead to conclusions that might be expressed like this: it is not monotheism as such, but a particular *use* of it that makes it a function of a view of society in which order and the common good are assured by a sovereign will (whether this be of a ruler, a group or a class). Furthermore, the root of ideology, of the false understanding that covers self-interest with a justificatory veneer of ideas, never resides in an inner necessity of religious imagination, but in a will to power that makes that imagination an organic function of an interest. This means that neither monotheistic nor trinitarian orthodoxy, in themselves, escape the possibility of being taken over by a hollow ideology. This ideology takes over when religious imagination, whether belonging to a monotheistic religion or to the purest Christian trinitarian orthodoxy, is torn from its mystical horizon and functionally tied to an ethical outlook.

In order to try and clarify this assertion, let us freely take up some of the arguments in the theological methodology of 'Dionysius the Areopagite', particularly from his treatise on *Mystical Theology*. Dionysius there works out a reflection on religious language in which this is considered in relation to *union* with God. The term *mystical* here refers just to the experience of *enosis*—union. Theology is a product of mystical language because it develops a whole imagery and conceptual world expressed as a series of stages, involving a process of passing from the symbolic universe to denial of ultimate identity through God and symbol, of purifying one's ego and leading it to experience of the presence. The first stage of this process, which should lead to the place of presence, consists in the subjective awareness, the interiorisation (= affirmation) of the divine present in the world and in history. This is the monent when the divine comes down, when every object and every action is seen in its identity with its origins: fire, air, feelings, choices, imaginings: everything is a symbol of God. This is the stage at which the presence seems to exclude all absence, at which God is the Strong One, when Pharaoh's chariots sink in the mire which represents the misunderstanding of the symbolic nature of the world. But intoxication and dance, exaltation and freedom, the Promethean climb to the origins of fire and life, must all give way to negation, must recognise absence. The descent of the divine, in fact, which is the origin of religious imagining, is on its own the basis of the will to power, a pure strength in which the personality exalts itself and becomes proud. This means that the experience of *ek-stasis* is precluded, that the consciousness cannot expand to welcome otherness, the different destiny that cannot be reduced to what is mine. Not only this, but the descent of the divine, the fêting of identity, remain meaningless till they lead to the final achievement of the absence of the senses, of death, of hell. And there where the soul is abandoned by God, where it is faced with the ends that limit its passage through time, identity becomes an empty word, the basis of existence is withdrawn and the bottomless pit is opened. Can God make 'his' what is not 'his'?

Perhaps the uniqueness of God resides just in this: that he is in a position to assimilate what is outside him, that he can be in what what was not put there by him.

The place where it was not put by God, and where God can nevertheless be, has to be traversed by the soul that seeks to unite itself to God. This is the meaning of the earthly existence of Jesus of Nazareth. Here the 'descent' of God is finally consummated in the place where Jesus is abandoned by God. But here is the paradox; that God was precisely in that abandonment, in that absence. We now have to understand *this* identity, which is beyond all affirmation, in the 'most bright darkness' of the unconscious, of abandonment, where all religious imagery is burnt on the altar of the absolute communion imposed by accepting the destiny of another. Ascetic at first, conjoining with the Father is achieved in the end by 'negation' (*apophatic* theology). At the stage of mystical ascesis, which follows symbolic descent,

Dionysius goes on to say, every theological conception of God, however exalted, has to be abandoned, because God is elsewhere. And yet negation is not absolutised; the intoxication of symbols is not followed by the intoxication of destruction: God is beyond both affirmation and negation. Negation is not the resting-point, security; it is only purification through *ekstasis*, through communion, through the enjoyment of the presence. Our highest and most divine conceptions are only peaks on which the presence rests. This is the original world of religious imagery. It is a mystical universe. One of its constituent parts is ethics. Ethics comes into operation only when this way is interrupted and the need arises to divide, to separate, to abandon something to its destiny of damnation in order to save a part of ourselves and of our history: knowledge of good and evil.

In general, the ethical universe comes into being through building up the symbolic dimension, through an attempt to block and divide the descent of the divine, to give definitive and not merely dynamic dignity to an action: to do otherwise is to be damned. Ethics arises when one tries to provide a dwelling-place for the divine, which thus becomes the demonic force behind an existence: 'man's *ethos* is the devil', said the Greeks. And *ethos* means simply 'dwelling' or 'character'.

When man maps out walls in which God shall live, the divine becomes a project of existence and existence itself becomes sacralised. Then the *uniqueness* of God becomes a confine, the exclusion of everything that cannot be integrated into the project and, at the same time, the cohesive principle of everything that allows itself to be integrated into the project. The hardest question arises from the *inevitability* of ethics: why must knowledge of good and evil come about? Paul gives his reply, which is still extremely appealing: the law has to intervene between the original promise and the future grace of presence, as an interval, because it matches the radical diversity and superabundance of grace. In Paul, what we have called ethics, that is the Mosaic law and the moral law inscribed in heart of each one of us, is incapable of leading to God, so sin, that is separation from God and condemnation, multiplies. And yet law is not sin and itself comes from God. Its justification is that it is a 'pedagogue', that is a gaoler and a teacher at the same time. It is through the bankruptcy of the law that we are actually forced to experience the need for and the fulness of grace which is contained in the Gospel of Christ.

According to this Pauline view, the *ethos* would then be the necessary imprisonment of the divine in history, because man, precisely through the ethical experience and its bankruptcy, rediscovers the original meaning of the true way, the truth of religious imagination, the absence of symbols.

Paul's vision is not the only possible answer to the question of the meaning of ethics and its relationship to mysticism. Other answers can be found within the New Testament itself. Here I have tried only to give the broad outlines of his vision to show that even the Christian religious imagination does not possess an unchanging universe, but is susceptible of various collocations and can give rise to differing connections with human experience.

4. THE DREAM OF THE SECULARISED WEST

With the break-up of Christian unity within Western society in the sixteenth century, the accord between Christian faith and social ethics that had basically been inaugurated by the 'peace' of Constantine, began to fall apart. For some twelve centuries it had seemed possible to identity the horizon of the gospels, of the reconciliation between God and man proclaimed in Jesus Christ, with the ethical horizons of Western Christendom. This identification had till then seemed possible because the 'enemy' was then represented by those cut off from the Good News, the contemporary enemies of him who, on the Cross, had shown the presence of God even when he was far from God. The division among Christians which made it impossible from the sixteenth century on to think of the faith as making for unity within the same society, imposed instead the need to find a new balance for the social ethic. The State released itself from any reference to religious understanding, became 'absolute', looked for its own foundations. Prior to this, politics had already undergone a 'secularisation'—sufficient to recall Marsilio Ficino and Dante. But these were moves which still left the fusion of the Christian horizon and the political horizon intact, at least in principle, while seeking a different balance between the elements that made up society. With the sixteenth century any possible tie between the Gospel and politics was effectively loosened. But is an effectively 'secularised' basis for the State a possibility? Is it possible to base a social ethic on the criminal hypothesis that God does not exist? The answers to this question given by lawyers and historians are far from unanimous; they divide into several currents and often flatly contradict one another. For example, Carl Schmitt, whom Peterson attacked, put forward the thesis that the rulers who preside over modern social orders are still theological rulers, even if in a secularised form. So it is not possible, at least in the existing orders, to cut the umbilical cord which links politics to theology.

We are not concerned here with the theoretical political aspect of the question, but with its effect on the history of the Christian process. Christians who feel themselves responsible for the way of Jesus Christ in fact examine the question of the *uniqueness* of their witness first so as to guarantee the contribution it can make to human experience. This aspect leads to two considerations, one looking back to the past and one direct to the present; both refer mainly to the Roman Catholic Church, but perhaps concern other churches as well, at least in part.

(a) The Catholic Church has in the past viewed this attempt to separate ethics from the Gospel with suspicion and enmity, seeing it as a rebellion not only against the authority of the Church, but also against God, and an attempt to break up the social ethic as a whole, to subvert the principles by which all men live together. Now that modern secular democracies seem to be based on this separation, they too have, at least at their outset, been greeted with a suspicious rejection. To use the words of Pope Pius IX in his encyclical *Quanta cura*: 'when religion is alienated from civil society and, with the refusal of the doctrine and authority of divine revelation, the true notion of law and human justice is obscured and lost, and in place of true justice and legitimate right, material force is brought into play, then it becomes clear that some people, totally forgetful of the most certain principles of right reason and without a care for them, dare to proclaim: "The will of the people, shown by so-called public opinion or by some other means, constitutes the supreme law, loosed from all human and divine laws and, in the political order, events that have come to pass acquire the force of law simply because they have come to pass" '. In this ecclesial rejection, which was historically developed in the preamble to the Constitution *Dei Filius* of Vatican I by attributing the ultimate source of all this evil to the Protestant Reformation, the Church still failed to ask itself whether the separation between social ethic and Christian outlook, so often overlaid with polemical and desacralising overtones, should not in fact be laid at the door of the unjustified claims of the Church itself in taking on the last ditch defence of an organic connection between Christianity and politics which showed little respect for the otherness of the Gospel.

(b) In present times, the Church has gone back to being excessively sensitive to offers of new forms of *pax constantiniana* put forward by the ruling powers, even though these may not be State rulers in the strict sense, but new incarnations of social and political power. The request coming from many parts for religious principles to become once more the basis of the social contract show the persistence of a 'bourgeois religion', a religious imagination devoted to giving guarantees and security to *this* social order, thereby persistently de-eschatologising the basic values of the Christian tradition, as Metz has said. Modern Western societies are rediscovering a new actuality in the 'powers' of Christian institutions, such as perhaps have not been seen since the days of the Ancien Régime. The risk involved in this is that the Christian journey through history will take on the aspect of political Christianity, basically ethical, through which God's power to reclaim even 'what is not his' through the powerlessness and weakness of the Cross, his love for all that is human, will perhaps be taken over by absorption only of what the world recognises as his.

CONCLUSION: TWO WAYS OF LOOKING AT THE HUMANITY OF GOD

The ethical, social and political application of the uniqueness of God is often justified by appeal to the fact that God became man and that God has only one plan for man. But there are two ways of looking at this humanity of God. The first starts from the universal and moves to the particular. That is, it starts from an abstract conception of humanity, of nature, joined to a coherent view of history. The particularity of Christianity is then seen as the embodiment of this application and as the universal will of all creatures. The uniqueness of God, including that of the God of Jesus Christ, cannot but give place to the realisation of a universal principle. In some theological schemes this view goes so far as to affirm that the 'damnation of the individual' can be justified and willed in the universal, global perspective of the salvation of humanity.

The second approach starts from the particular and moves to the universal; that is, it starts from the evangelical beatitudes: blessed are you poor, for yours is the kingdom of heaven. The meaning of this promise can only be grasped if its 'theological' nature is understood. It is not in fact an invitation to poverty, but a statement of the place in which God has put himself so as to be *with* 'all' men: with those who are alienated *from* 'all'. Insufficient attention is generally paid to the fact that the company Jesus kept was in the first place a company of sinners, of those who were thereby cut off from God himself. Here God's humanity is one of radical companionship, knocking down all dividing walls.

The first approach fails to eliminate the (ethical) notion of the enemy, and is the root of all the integralisms of so-called Christian politics, Christian culture, Christian society, etc. The second approach seeks to live the poverty of God in history through joyous or suffering participation in the joy or suffering of each and every individual, without being able to boast of bearing with it the religious 'foundation' for ethical and political actions.[3]

Translated by Paul Burns

Notes

1. L. Massignon *La Passion de Husayn Ibn Mansûr Hallâj* (Paris, 1975, 4 vols); *idem*, 'Perspective transhistorique sur la vie de Hallâj' in *Parole donnée* (Paris 1962) pp. 73–97.

2. See in particular E. Peterson 'Zeuge der Wahrheit' in *Theologische Traktate* (Munich 1951) pp. 165–224.

3. For further bibliographical indications, and a more complete examination of the views put forward here, may I refer to my own writings: *La compagnia della fede. Linee de teologia fondamentale* (Turin 1980) pp. 109–165; 'Resistenza e dogma; il rifiuto di qualsiasi ideologia politica in Erik Peterson' in *E. Peterson. Il monoteismo come problema politico* (Brescia 1983) pp. 5–26; with I. Mancini *Fede e cultura* (Turin 1979) pp. 49–83; with R. Orfei, F. Stame, G. Piana *La necessità dell'inutile: fede e politica* (Turin 1982) pp. 7–43.

Michel Meslin

The Anthropological Function of Monotheism

IN A study of the anthropological function of monotheism, the basic question to be discussed is whether belief in one God distinct from the world contributed to the individualisation of believing man. In other words, we have to examine whether the emphasis monotheism placed on some idea of divine transcendence, experienced by man as the exercise of a creative, organising and sovereign power, led to the emergence of individual relations between man, inserted as he is in a socialised and ritualised space, and a Beyond where the Other dwells. And if so, did these relations result in development of the idea of the person?

This notion of the person is not an easy one to grasp. It is neither obvious nor a matter of plain fact, and there have been many human societies, some still in existence today, where it never emerged as a basic organisational element. In societies of this kind, man exists only in the plural; the individual is simply a numerical fragment of the ethnic or social group, and the only imaginable relations between men and the divine are necessarily mediated by the group. An individual can only reach the divinity through the socio-political structures; his relations with the divine, therefore, are based on the anthropocentric ideas of contract or covenant that govern relations between men.

Now, analysis has shown that the religious factor was probably not a primary cause in the slow process of development, in the West, of the idea of the person. Rather, the first impulse was given when society granted the individual certain rights and prerogatives, and hence certain responsibilities; what allowed the individual gradually to attain the dignity of a human person was the role he played in the organisation of the city or group and the legal status he enjoyed.[1]

The aspiration to individuality did, however also appear in the religious sphere. A first, very anthropocentric sign of it was the *daimôn*, the *genius*, the *anima*, divine representations fabricated by man to figure his most inward self, that which makes the individual an individual, the living spark proper to each man, which makes each man a unique and individual sum of qualities and behaviour thought of as divine gifts.

Again, in ancient and traditional societies, to fulfil a role in religious rituals, in sacrifices or brotherhood festivals, detaches man from the group and gives him autonomy in his relations with the divine. The sheer face of wearing a mask and playing a role makes him cease to be a mere numerical element of the group. He really is the *persona*; he is the mask, the god's companion, the part of the totem.

Yet again, the importance attached to individual trials in initiative rites, or recourse to divinatory practices in which the individual questions the divinity about his future, certainly helped to strengthen a more personal conception of the individual. In some of these societies, the fact that sickness and catastrophe can apparently only be explained by a fault or breach of a taboo shows that individual responsibility was a very important basic factor in the notion of the person.

Finally, there are the philosophers, poets and sages, with their reflections on man's place in the world. They went back to the content of the old myths and asked whether the individual could, as an individual, be free and independent in his relations both with other men and with the world of the divine.

However, it is clear that the development even of monotheistic metaphysical theories contributed to the individualising process only in so far as they had an effect in practice on man's status, and led to individual relationships between believing man and the God whose unicity they affirmed. Thus, the monotheism of certain Presocratics, Xenophanes of Colophon for example, criticised anthropomorphic representations of God (*fr.* 23–25), we cannot however be sure that this monotheism—whatever its significance at another level—did actually resituate Greek man in relation to God. The 'first to postulate a Unity', as Aristotle called Xenophanes, cannot be hailed as the first champion of the human person, doubtless because he did not differentiate between the 'One God, motionless and at rest in himself' and the world of nature and matter (*fr.* 28). When Heraclitus, for his part, affirmed the omnipotence of the eternal Logos which rules the world and to which man is closely bound (*fr.* 72), he pointed out that what makes the human condition tragic is that men 'live as if they had a private understanding, whereas the Logos is common to all' (*fr.* 2). Affirmation of the unicity of God is thus paralleled by statement of the tragic situation of man, who lives in appearances and can neither hear nor speak, rent between the Being that is the only Wise and the existence which constitutes him (*fr.* 32).

The earliest Greek affirmations of monotheism, then, remain at the level of philosophical theory. Even if, like W. Jaeger, one thinks that the Presocratics laid the first foundations of a natural theology, worked out a mode of knowledge and worshipped the divine, this does not mean that they radically altered the human situation in the Greek world.[2] The cities of the Eleatics were not a paradise where the human person grew to strength. And it was ethical meditation on the place of man in the world, not philosophical proclamation of monotheism, that allowed the rudiments of the notion of person to emerge in Greek antiquity.

The spread of Wisdom cults from the Near East marked the beginning of a new stage, first in the Hellenic and then in the Roman world. The mystery cults altered the traditional view of the sacred quite drastically; they developed the idea of divine transcendence, but by doing so within a polytheistic framework of religious representations, they changed the type of—often contractual—relations that hitherto had governed men's dealings with the divine powers. Political unification of the Mediterranean world caused its gods to merge: under different names, one single divinity was now the object of honour, the one in which the powers and functions of all the rest were concentrated; the various names merely symbolised different kinds of relationship with men. The effect of this concentration of functions was to give the supreme deity absolute sovereignty over the world and time, beings and things. In a recent and quite outstanding study based on detailed analysis of epigraphic documents,[3] it has been shown that recourse to a God termed *Hypsistos* revealed a refinement in the conception of deity; more particularly, the study shows that this deity was not simply a matter of speculation on the part of intellectuals or theologians, but the object of a real devotion which spread, through very varied social milieux, to affect most of the eastern part of the Roman world. The study demonstrates clearly how the divine name became depersonalised in proportion as the divine figure was thought of and experienced by believing man as more abstract and universal. So divine transcendence developed outside the traditional ritual specifications. At the same time however, parallel to the *basileia*, the divine sovereignty, there developed a universal fatherhood which brought out the essential link between monotheism and creation. This link was to become a commonplace of religious thinking at the end of the Greco-Roman period.[4]

This development, which is of major importance in the religious history of the first centuries of our era, was contemporary with the spread of the oriental mystery cults. These cults matched an existential anguish in believing man that the traditional religious forms could no longer assuage; they thus demonstrated clearly the felt need for a more personal relationship with the deity with which man strives for union. Their ethic was sometimes demanding and their initiatic experiences often redoubtable; they exploited sensibility and affectivity, and used the attraction of mystery to stimulate the imagination; the kind of religious experience they offered apprehended the divine through man and grasped it sensibly and immediately. Thus they wanted of their followers a will to moral and psychical purification, to be achieved through ritual actions the strict fulfilment of which had soteriological value. From such orthopraxis there follows a valorisation of present time, in which man can act to make himself as much 'like the god' as possible.

It must here be pointed out that like that of the Greek philosophers, though attained of course by very different paths, the perfection offered by the mystery cults was still basically anthropocentric, even in the ideal of the *homoiôsis théô*, being like the god. To the devotee who made the efforts required by initiation and by the 'commandments' Julian mentions in relation to the cult of Mithra, they taught that by totally fulfilling himself man became more himself. In so doing, they were initiating a religious process of development of the person which is primarily that which, in man, reveals itself to man by constant and conscious possession of his faculties and virtualities. The cults' call to constantly transcend man and his limitations is accompanied by the promise of a kind of happiness that is more or less sublimated into a still somewhat vague concept of salvation. Such was the high point of the whole of ancient religious anthropology. But it could not reach beyond this point. For these religious experiences could not reveal the face of a saving god who intervened in each individual human destiny, and so they never became a saving religion.[5]

To sum up, the end product of the religious development of pagan antiquity was recognition of the unicity of a divine Power to which man could relate by a variety of ritual paths that, henceforth, were more independent of the social and political structures. The importance of this achievement cannot be denied; *stricto sensu*, however, it cannot be said to constitute a personalising monotheism.

A similar picture will emerge from what must be a quick glance at traditional black African societies, which are so much closer to us in time. In many ways the African world is a perfect example of the kind of all-embracing religious experience in which the sacred pervades the whole of life and there are close links between, on the one hand, the visible world of men and things, and the invisible world on the other. The latter, ordered by a God which created it, is activated by powers which, under various names, represent the different functions and manifestations of the one God. Subtending all these relations is the vital energy in which all beings share.

The African religious system thus emerges as a hierarchised structure, at least as regards its most widespread features. At the top is a supreme Being, usually inaccessible, which after creating the world more or less withdrew from it: a *deus otiosus* which has everything it requires, and has therefore no need of men's worship or prayers. It has not totally abandoned men however, but left them the genies and fetishes to help and guide them. African animism thus in no way conflicts with recognition of a God who is Lord, transcendent, and the one source of life; it merely shows how important the idea of mediation is in African thinking.[6] However, it cannot be denied that in practice, with the exception of some theologians who have reached the peaks of initiation and some sages like Ogotemmêli who talked with Marcel Griaule, Africans in general tend not to know of the supreme God.[7] The basic monotheism is obscured by the animist and fetishist ritual practices, and it is fair to say that in these traditional African societies, God remains beyond man's grasp—the God who is called only by an indeterminate name, 'the Great Name', 'the Great One', or indeed, among the Giziga of North Cameroon, 'the Master of the forgotten'.

Reverting to God's withdrawal from the world: according to a large number of myths, it took place after man transgressed a divine command. It usually figures therefore as the dramatic condition of man's emergence as he is *hic et nunc* in the world. Thus 'everything begins as theology and ends as anthropology' as R. Jaouen has aptly said in a commentary on the withdrawal of God in the myths of North Cameroon, according to which it was man who drove God from earth.[8] But this distant God is also close, through the secondary deities that 'stand in' for him, but also through the wisdom daily diffused by the myths that are the standard to which all human actions are referred. He is accessible to African man in a personal mode too, in the slow search for God within initiation societies. D. Zahan has used the example of the Bambara to show how the initiation process leads to knowledge of the God who is Lord and to a veritable deification of man, at the outcome of rituals—which are very similar to those of the ancient mystery cults—in which the neophyte is put to death, interred in a symbolic grave, and born anew.[9] The reborn man must then grow and mature, since he does not yet possess the totality of the *Ni*, the unconscious substrate of the *Dya*, i.e. of his *genius*, his own being. The initiate is thus called to attain perfection in his relations with God and possession of all the divine principles, in an experience of identification with God that is a true mystical experience.

In this African context, which from some points of view is so like that of the mediterranean world in antiquity, the notion of person emerges as a very complex reality. It is the sum of all the individual's relations with the world, the visible world in which he lives and the invisible world in which he shares by his vital energy. For African man's most authentic religious experience points him towards establishing an individual relationship with his cosmic and social environment as well as with a God who is both close and far off, in order to realise his own being as fully as possible. In black Africa, then, as in other human societies, the person is never a natural datum, but emerges as the product of a history proper to each individual, 'of an *I-with* that is awareness of self, of the other and of the Wholly Other'.[10]

This brief analysis of pagan antiquity and African societies shows clearly that in any strictly creationist mythology, the organisation of the world and of life, including man's, is explicitly attributed to a transcendent God. The resulting natural order is then the basis of the moral system that underlies communal life and religious experience, and develops in the individual a kind of existential realism. For this created world order leads to attitudes governed by a kind of exchange, in which as a 'counter-gift' man observes his creator's law. The individual must accept his condition as a limited and finite being because that is the will of God. But it does not follow that this conscious acceptance of the *ordo rerum* enables personalising relations to develop between the believer and his God, since simple creationism usually places the creator of all things outside the very structure that man is wholly involved in; a God-figure inevitably suffers if it becomes *otiosus* once its task as creator has been fulfilled.

Man may thus very well have two strictly parallel conceptions of the divine: as immanent in the life of beings and things which God once upon a time created, and as transcendent but so far distant that nothing can now link man to it. There can only be a real possibility of relations between God and his creatures if God the creator is, and remains, continuing life in each of them. To the transcendent and creator God must therefore be adjoined a Providence which has the watchfulness of love and does not stand outside its creation. God must be wholly inserted in the world, must agree to assume the whole condition of the world and of man whom he created in his own image: only on this condition can there be new relations between God and men. And it was precisely this that was new and revolutionary about the Judaeo-Christian faith.

As Paul Tillich has shown, the personalism originated by biblical monotheism is set clearly apart from other religions by its doctrine of creation that is fulfilled in the Incarnation of the divine Word in the person of Jesus, the Christ.[11] And indeed if man—man in the world—is a realisation of the thought of a transcendent God, and if the Logos of God is his Son, then we must admit that there is no essential difference between the divine structure of the cosmos as it is perceptible to man, and the cosmic dimension of the Son of God, the incarnate Word 'by Whom all things were made'. The very notion of incarnation thus writes into human history a God who is encounter, encounter between a Person who is present and who acts in the world through other persons, and forges individual relations with them.

Now, what is distinctive about biblical religious experience is the use, along with other psycho-sociological representations, of the image of the father to express the historically experienced relations between Israel and its God. There is then a parental relation linking Yahweh and Israel 'his first-born son' whom 'he brought out of the land of Egypt' (Exodus 4:22; 20:2) and 'drew with affection and love' in order to make it an adult people (Hosea 11:1–4). This love of Yahweh is indeed a paternal love, in the sense that it does not originate with the son or his merits, but with God alone, and cannot be lost even if the son is unworthy of it. At the time of Hellenistic Judaism, the transcendent God was invoked as 'Lord, Father and sovereign Ruler of my life' (*Sirach* 23:1–4), a clear sign of a more personal religion in which Yahweh was God-Father not only of his chosen people, but also of each individual pious Jew. His fatherhood was then associated with the idea of *pronoïa*, Providence (Wisdom 14:3), and this theme foreshadowed that of the universalism of the fatherhood of God present in the world by his Wisdom, a theme Philo of Alexandria was to spell out.

At this point it must be stated very clearly that just as no man can claim to have his origin in himself, so God cannot be named by man. His fatherhood is merely an image, a metaphor, representing Him who has revealed himself as Being, the 'I am'. This symbolic God-Father figure is rooted in man's symbolary and based on a fundamental experience. It sets up a close connection, in any individual existence, between apprehension of God and fatherhood. But this analogy between human fatherhood and divine fatherhood can never be complete; in no way does it define the Being of God.[12] The relation between the two kinds of fatherhood is really that of a functional analogy. God is perceived, as a human father is, as master, sage, judge, powerful, giver of life. And when a believer says 'God and Father', he is defining his own behaviour towards God, not the Being of God. Only God can name himself, and name his creature: it is that act of absolute paternal recognition that a believer is confessing when he says 'Abba!' As a child derives its existence from its father, takes its name from him and learns freedom from him, so, in God-Father, the believer recognises the existence of a Being who speaks to him and calls him by his name during his own personal history. 'Father' is in fact an echo that harks back to the name God himself gives himself in his work of creation and in his Incarnation; it is also a recognition of the real and individual bonds that unite man to God.[13]

The deep import of the parental relation that joins man to God through so personal a bond as that of filiation may be thought to be that it reveals, to every man, how personal God is, personal to the extent that man can encounter him in every individual existence. By becoming incarnate, God assumes each human person totally. Now, since Paul (1 Corinthians 3:9 and 2 Corinthians 6:1), Christian anthropology has always stressed that God's creatures are called to cooperate in his saving work. The importance of this mission gives everyone the dimension of a responsible person, a dimension which is shown by the possibility of communicating to others the essence of one's individual being, one's own consciousness, i.e. an intelligence and an independent will.

The idea of man's responsible autonomy within creation was in part a heritage of Stoicism, and its importance had been emphasised by Justin;[14] however, one of the earliest and best formulations of it is to be found in the early fifth century *Letter to Demetrias* by Pelagius. In this letter Pelagius develops the idea of the high value of man, the masterwork of God, who gave man the unique privilege of reason, i.e. awareness of his acts (*Ad Dem.* 3). Now, it is reason that enables him to know God and that makes him, alone in the universe, the only freely willing and wholly unconstrained executor of divine justice. It enables him to discern good from evil, and so leaves him the chance to merit salvation by himself. For the possibility of disobeying God's law is the *sine qua non* of the freedom that constitutes human dignity. The immense importance of a text that sets man in a relation of total freedom with God—and that so great a dignity is bestowed on his creature proves God's infinite goodness—will readily be appreciated. Augustine contested its teaching vigorously, but it was destined to be more fully and more judiciously developed by Aquinas, according to whom only a human person with the gift of reason could glorify God through knowledge and love.[15] But as we know, Pelagianism fiercely rejected any idea of moral weakness caused by original sin, and so rapidly came to teach an unrealistically optimistic glorification of human nature. In Pelagius himself, however, this exaltation of the responsibility that goes with human freedom underlies a constant invitation to the individual perfection whereby man attains complete development. For if he so wishes, a man who has chosen virtue can reach the stage of living in total union with God: 'There is a breath of heaven about the body . . . I think there are men in whom God dwells'.[16]

This religious anthropology, that combines the sense of freedom—inherited from the Greeks—that is needed for full human development, the idea of contractual relations with God, and exaltation of the Creator and the goodness of his work, was in part to be taken up by Thomism. But in the sixteenth and seventeenth centuries, when man was being rediscovered in the West in the light of the Reformation, and a new Christian humanism was being worked out, Jansenism quickly reimposed a more Augustinian view of relations between man and God, leaving no room for Pelagian optimism. Today on the contrary, this optimism can perhaps be seen at work again, not in theological form but underlying behavioural patterns both individual and collective, and encouraging an accommodative ethic. For in as much as it is the basis of an ontology of freedom, Pelagian optimism is one of the most fundamental trends in Christian anthropology.

It will not be irrelevant to our theme to recall that in the most absolute of the Abrahamic monotheisms, that of the Koran, man's election is affirmed no less clearly: 'we have given nobility to the sons of Adam'.[17] God chose imperfect man to be his representative (*khalifa*) on earth rather than the angels, his obedient servants. But man only completely fulfils this representative function if he is faithful to his mission of witness to the One. He tries therefore to admire the flawless harmony of creation and read there the signs of God that proclaim the Omnipotence and goodness of the All-High. 'Lord, you did not create all this in vain', cries the believer who has been given the world in trust, and has been given also the imperative duty both to reflect and reason, and to act in order to bring justice and peace to the world. This summons to responsibility naturally implies that in his daily life, the believer will be faithful to the Law and will remain aware of the fleeting nature of human action, 'for all things perish, save the face of God'.[18]

This, then, in a necessarily brief survey, is the anthropological function of monotheism, a locus and cause of the development of a personal relationship between man and the One All-Powerful. History shows that once the idea of the human person is accepted and is recognised *de facto*, whether or not it is explicitly formulated in law, it begins to operate as an effective factor for change and development—though not always for progress—within society. It is as if the individual, who can influence social, political and economic realities only as a member of a given group, drew from his capacity as a person the freedom and strength he needs to reject and sometimes to break away from collective constraints and the tyranny of the social. Contemporary experience shows clearly that the value of the human person transcends any political society, whatever its coercive powers. It shows even more clearly that only the definition and justification conferred on the limits of the person by a religious faith can give it even greater eminence and dynamism. As Simone Weil so aptly wrote: 'Only by entering the transcendent, the supernatural and the authentically spiritual does man rise above the social'.[19]

Translated by Ruth Murphy

Notes

1. *Problèmes de la personne* directed by I. Meyerson E.P.H.E., 6th section (Paris 1973).

2. W. Jaeger *The Theology of the Early Greek Philosophers* (Oxford 1947).

3. N. Belaÿche *Les Divinites Hypsistos* unpublished thesis. Summary in *Dieu et Dieux, noms et Nom* (Angers 1983) pp. 37–47.

4. Maximus of Tyre *Diss.* XVII.5; Philo *De spec.leg.* II, 165, etc.

5. For a fuller discussion of these themes see my article 'Realités psychiques et valeurs religieuses dans les cultes orientaux' in *Revue Historique* 512 (Oct–Dec 1974) 289–314.

6. See Amadou Hampaté Ba in *Les Religions africaines traditionelles. Recontres internationales de Bouaké* (Paris 1965) pp. 33–55.

7. *Dieu d'eau* (Paris 1966).

8. R. Jaouen 'Le Mythe de la retraite de Bumbulvun' in *La Nomination de Dieu, Afrique et Parole* no. 33–34 p. 56.

9. D. Zahan *Sociétés d'initiation Bambara, le N'domo, le Koré* (Paris 1960) and *Religion, spiritualité et pensée africaines* (Paris 1970).

10. J. M. Agossou 'Anthropologie africaine et la notion de personne' in *L'Expérience religieuse africaine et les relations interpersonelles*, ICAO (Abidjan 1982) p. 239.

11. P. Tillich *Biblical Religion and the Search for Ultimate Reality* (Chicago 1955).

12. See P. Rocoeur 'La Paternité, du fantasme au symbole' in *Herméneutique et Psychanalyse* (Paris 19??).

13. M. Meslin 'Dieu et Père' in *Dieu et dieux, noms et Nom* (Angers 1983) pp. 13–23.

14. Justin *2 Apol.* VII,6: 'Any creature is capable of good and of evil and would have no merit if it could not choose between the two ways'.

15. *Summa Theologia* 1a, qq. 29–32.

16. *De Virginitate*, 12.

17. *Koran* 17, 70.

18. *Koran* 28, 88. See L. Gardet *Les Hommes de l'Islam* (Paris 1977) p. 49ff.

19. S. Weil *La Pesanteur et la grâce*, p. 184.

PART II

Theological Reflection

Bernhard Lang

No God but Yahweh! The Origin and Character of Biblical Monotheism

1. JOSIAH'S REFORM AND ITS PREHISTORY

BIBLICAL SCHOLARS usually agree that monotheism was first set forth not with Abraham or Moses, but under Josiah. In 622 BC a scroll was brought to the Judean King Josiah (641–609) and read out to him. The book (allegedly discovered during the restoration of the Jerusalem Temple) contained a cultic code which no one until then had followed and which overthrew all previous codes. It demanded the abolition of the cults of all divinities other than Yahweh, who was the only one who might be worshipped in the Temple at Jerusalem. The High Priest Hilkiah, high-ranking officials and a prophetess consulted on the matter supported the book, and Josiah made it the law of the State.

Judah now had a written codification of its religion, of a kind known in comparative religion as 'monolatrous'. Perhaps other gods and goddesses existed, but Judah was to worship only its national God, Yahweh. Even if the king's reformation was less stringent that the biblical narrative says, it nevertheless gives a good idea of Israel's traditional *poly*theistic religion. 'And he deposed the idolatrous priests . . . who burned incense to Baal, to the sun, and the moon, and the constellations, and all the host of the heavens' (2 Kings 23:5).

It is generally accepted today that the reforming code of law constitutes the basis of Deuteronomy. It is more difficult to decide the age and origin of the retrieved text. Perhaps the find was only a pious fraud, and the ink on the scroll was scarcely dry when it was read to the king.

41

But the Yahweh-alone movement behind the book was no new thing. Our possession of a historical work indebted to the Deuteronomic body of thought enables us to reconstruct that movement's image of its own history. The Yahweh-alone movement saw itself as beginning in the mists of prehistory, in the legendary time of Moses. Yahweh had revealed himself to Moses and had given him his law. Although it is impossible to determine exactly when Moses and his successor Joshua lived, we can discern a sequence of more or less distinctly historical events:

(a) In the ninth-century northern kingdom of Israel there was a fierce confrontation between a Yahweh-alone movement and worshippers of a god called Baal. King Ahab (874–853) supported Baal-worship, but the prophet Elijah opposed it, King Jehoram (852–834) restricted it, and Jehu (841–813) finally got rid of it altogether.

(b) In the eighth century, Hosea, a northern-kingdom prophet, became a very strong advocate of the exclusive worship of Yahweh. Hosea, to be sure, is not mentioned in the Deuteronomic history, but the spirit and language of Deuteronomy itself are indebted to him.

(c) In the southern kingdom, King Hezekiah of Judah (728–699) introduced a cultic reform which satisfied major demands of the Yahweh-alone movement. He destroyed the places where other gods were worshipped, broke up idols, and cleansed the Jerusalem Temple of pagan accretions.

Biblical criticism has expended a great deal of ingenuity on establishing a prehistory of Josiah's reform. Unfortunately the results are only provisional and still contested by researchers. Moses is taken to be a historical figure and is probably to be located in the thirteenth century BC He possibly introduced worship of Yahweh. But the Yahweh-alone idea seems to be alien to him. Many people have heard of Sigmund Freud's psychoanalytical midrash *Moses and Monotheism* (1939); Freud claimed to detect in the religion of Yahweh an echo of the fourteenth-century Egyptian belief in Aton. Admittedly Psalm 104 must be indebted to religious verse of the Egyptian Amarna period, but Freud's thesis has been abandoned as outdated. The study is still valuable as an analysis of a religious father-figure. But it is invalid as a contribution to the history of monotheism. Like the form taken by his religion, the figure of Moses is still obscured by the usual shadows of religious origins. Joshua's covenant discourse at a tribal assembly at Schechem is just as much a product of pious fantasy as the night-time destruction of a pagan temple related in the books of the Judges (Josh. 24; Judg. 6:25–32). Moses' successors also live in the shadowland of legend and have not yet emerged into the light of history.

Unfortunately ninth-century events are almost as obscure. King Ahab's wife Jezebel, a princess from the Phoenician city of Sidon, would seem to have introduced alien cults. Why and by whom these were resisted we do not know. Perhaps the new temples attracted a vast number of people so that the old places of worship lost out financially. Economic envy can occur in the world of religions too. We have no idea what course the conflict ran. The most assured fact is the removal of a cultic symbol dedicated to Baal from the Samarian capital. King Joram (852–841) is said to have done this. In 841 Jehu usurped his throne. King Jehu had Jezebel (by now Ahab's widow) murdered, and killed the Baal worshippers. Perhaps that indicates his withdrawal from a foreign policy orientated to Sidon and Tyre. Jehu was more interested in Assyria. A stele in the British Museum shows Jehu kneeling before the Assyrian monarch Shalmaneser, and paying tribute to him. With Jezebel's death the close connection with Phoenicia came to an end; perhaps the Assyrians had already been implicated in Jehu's usurpation. According to the biblical accounts the Baal cult was rejected because worship of Yahweh alone was the ideal. But the existence of any such idea in the ninth century is improbable.

In the book of the prophet Hosea, who lived c. 750 BC in the northern kingdom, we find the first clear statement of a requirement of worship of Yahweh alone: 'I am the Lord your God from the land of Egypt; you know no God but me, and besides me there is no saviour' (Hos. 13:4). What a Jew or Christian would take as a reference to the Decalogue is rather the basis of the much later Ten Commandments, which in their turn depend on the statement in Hosea. Clearly only a small group advocated Yahwistic monolatry in the time of Hosea. The official Temple religion was not interested in the novelty: '. . . they kept sacrificing to the Baals and burning incense to idols' (Hos. 11:2). On several occasions it is obvious that worship of Yahweh alone is an extension and intensification of the struggle against Baal waged in the previous century. The 'other gods' are merely called 'the Baals'. 'And I will punish her for the feast-days of the Baals when she burned incense to them' is one Hosean assertion; and another says: 'I will remove the names of the Baals from her mouth' (Hos. 15, 19). The opposition was no longer merely to the Baal of Sidon, but to *all* local manifestations of Baal. Wherever Baal was worshipped, the Yahweh-alone movement rejected the cult. Of course the same was true of other gods who did not belong to the Baal type (the plague god, the death god, the love goddess, and so on). The express reference to the Baals is probably attributable not so much to the popularity of Baal shrines but much more to memory of the 'original conflict' in the ninth century between supporters of Yahweh and those of Sidonian Baal. Accordingly all gods are denounced as 'Baals'—as (alleged) competitors of Yahweh.

Under King Hezekiah of Judah we find the first trace in the southern kingdom of the influence of the Yahweh-alone idea. After the disappearance of the northern kingdom (722), a few people who belonged to the movement possibly came to Jerusalem, and soon found supporters there. Hezekiah is credited with an ambitious cultic reform (2 Kings 18:4); its historical basis, however, is modest. The king had a sacred tree (Hebr. *asherah*) and a bronze serpent removed from the Temple. That produced an imageless Yahweh cult in the Temple. The reason for the reform is not known. Perhaps the measure was taken under pressure from the Yahweh-alone movement during the Assyrian military invasion, when there was reason to fear that the southern kingdom would fall as the northern one had done. In that case more protection would have been expected from the Yahweh of iconless worship than from a god whose strength was represented by cultic symbols. Obviously iconoclasm was part of the programme of the Yahweh-alone movement, and people began to follow it, though perhaps only in times of need.

2. THE BREAKTHROUGH TO MONOTHEISM[1]

With the death (or murder?) of Josiah in 609, the last outstanding period of the Jewish monarchy came to an end. Once again sacrifice was offered to 'Baal, the sun, and the moon, and the constellations, and all the hosts of the heavens'. The Yahweh-alone movement, however, had taken such firm hold that it was no longer possible to suppress it. In the last years of the monarchy it found eloquent spokesmen in the prophets Jeremiah and Ezekiel. Both came from priestly families, were grounded in the Yahweh-alone movement of the time of Josiah, and carried the monolatrous idea into Babylonian exile. In Jeremiah we can observe an important development of the divine image. The prophet sees Yahweh as the creator of the world: 'It is I who by my great power and my outstretched arm have made the earth, with the men and animals that are on the earth, and I give it to whomever it seems right to me' (Jer. 27:5). This statement of 594 depicts Yahweh in the image of the Babylonian creator-god Marduk. At the same time the God of Israel bestows the overlordship of the world on the Babylonian King Nebuchadnezzar. Yahweh has been elevated to the rank of Creator with dominion over the world and is already almost the universal God of monotheism.

A generation after Jeremiah, the anonymous prophet whom we call Deutero-Isaiah completed the concept. The benevolent rule of the Persians having replaced Babylonian imperialism, Deutero-Isaiah acknowledges the Persian King Cyrus as the 'Messiah' appointed by Yahweh. But for the first time he sees Yahweh himself as the *one and only God*, besides whom there are no other gods. An encounter with the very old monotheistic religion of Zoroaster, which was widespread among the Persians, would seem to have given the prophet this idea. The Jews living in the Persian empire discovered a related faith in the Zoroastrian religion, which won considerable respect among them. Indeed, in their own religion the Jews now found several related teachings and customs and thereafter stressed them specially: the doctrine of creation, the uniqueness of God, and the significance of purity and dietary laws. Even in the sixth century there were sporadic Jewish echoes of the Zoroastrian doctrines of the next world and the resurrection. In this case they were even prepared to adopt new teachings from the cognate religion; these, however, took hold only centuries later.

Under the influence of Deutero-Isaiah, monotheism also entered Deuteronomy and the Deuteronomic history. Monotheistic statements were inserted when these writings took final shape (see Deut. 4:35: '. . . the Lord is God; there is no other besides him'). The corresponding revision was consciously made as the last possible; henceforth '. . . you shall not add to it or take from it' (Deut. 12:32). Not even prophets were allowed to propose any new doctrines.

The monotheistic profession of faith became the yardstick for the formation of the biblical canon. It could adopt only what was compatible with the Yahweh-alone idea or its advanced form, monotheism. Everything else was transformed in the process of revision, or thrown out. The Old Testament canon therefore contains only a few testimonies to the old polytheistic belief. In the story of paradise, we find the term for God, 'Yahweh Elohim'. This reminds us that the story originally recognised only the creator god Elohim, who was distinct from Yahweh but later equated with him: hence the unique occurrence of the two names. Lady Wisdom is a poetic image in the first nine chapters of Proverbs; earlier she would appear to have been an independent goddess of some significance for the body of higher officials. Finally, the name 'Shaddai', which is used for Yahweh, originally referred to the guardian god of individual and home. A trace of that is still apparent in the Jewish door amulet, the *mezuzah*, which contains a piece of parchment in a scroll inscribed with verses from the Bible and the name 'Shaddai' (protector God).

With Deutero-Isaiah and the Deuteronomic literature of the sixth (and possibly the fifth) century, we reach the end of a development which had begun some 300 years before. Now Judaism possessed its monotheistic creed, which it bore unaltered through history, to be handed on to Christianity and Islam. Monotheism is the gift to mankind of the religion of the Bible.

After this attempt to sketch the evolution of monotheism, it is time to look into its principles. How was it that the State deity of a small, politically and culturally insignificant nation reached the status of universal God?

3. FROM STATE GOD TO THE UNIVERSAL GOD OF MONOTHEISM

Polytheistic religions are also acquainted with the idea of the worship of one particular god and no other. Hence the position of Yahweh as Israel's national god was uncontested. All surrounding nations had *one* god for country and nation—the Moabites worshipped Chemosh, the Ammonites Milcom, the Assyrians Ashur, and the Egyptians Amon-Re. Micah 4:5 sums up the principle of the national god thus: 'for all the peoples walk each in the name of its god, but we will walk in the name of the Lord our God for ever and ever'. These national gods are especially concerned with war and peace, military supremacy, the well-being of monarchs, and so forth. In polytheistic Israel, however, other gods and goddesses were worshipped who were responsible for female fertility, family health and prosperity, wind and weather and so on; each therefore had his or her allotted area of responsibility.

Nevertheless, the special position of certain individuals made them interested only in the worship of Yahweh. That, however, did not mean that they enjoyed an exclusive relationship with this God, let alone demanded that of others. These people included the Davidic royal house, which had a special relationship with Yahweh and indeed had also built a temple for him directly by the Jerusalem palace. Among them above all were the prophets of Yahweh: for a man (or a woman) called by Yahweh to be his spokesman and messenger could have no great interest in other gods. No prophet can serve two masters simultaneously—say, Yahweh and Baal. For the same reason it was easy for the Yahweh-alone movement to arrogate the books of Yahweh prophets to itself, or even to rework them in its own favour. Amos and Isaiah were prophets of Yahweh: that is, they prophesied only in the name of Yahweh. They offered no messages from other gods. Although they themselves honoured only Yahweh—'. . . the Lord alone will be exalted . . .' (Isa. 2:11)— they showed no sign of demanding worship of Yahweh alone. Probably the most appropriate description of their faith is 'polytheistic'.

One circumstance makes it easier to pick Yahweh out of the gods worshipped in Palestine. Yahweh is distinctive in having no relatives in the world of the gods. He is neither the son of another god, nor has he any wife or descendants.[2] What exactly does that mean?

Every god has characteristics and a history which is narrated about him. The fact that Yahweh can not only become the opponent of other gods, but also is the opponent of *all* gods, must be grounded in his nature as unfolded and explained in myth. Eastern mythology, however, usually tells not merely of one god alone but of several deities who are associated in various ways. The usual form of connection is marriage, family and kinship. Like human beings, the gods do not appear as isolated individuals but are encountered in a network of kinship. The Egyptian Isis is Osiris' wife and Horus' mother—to name only one example. Apart from this genealogical form of organisation, mythology also features the divine state with a king, parliamentary body and hierarchy, especially among the Sumerians. The Old Testament also acknowledges the notion of a heavenly court, but this is incidental (1 Kings 22:19; Job 1:6). Yahweh appears as the outsider and loner who stands apart from the usual associations. Yahweh is a childless and unmarried God.

Researchers into pre-Islamic religion have constantly reported the existence of childless gods: they are described as *abtar*, which means 'without a son'. As a lonely god of this kind, Yahweh has little to do with the highly structured world of Canaanite deities. Whoever worships Yahweh does not have to honour the entire range of divinities at one and the same time, for Yahweh is related to none of them.[3] His claim to power will not make anyone his rival. No cousin will wax great in his shadow; no son will involve him in a conflict of the generations and take his place in the end. In societies with kin forms of organisation, special claims by individuals are usually treated by relations with little or no respect. The saying that a prophet is not honoured in his own country indicates the egalitarian ideal of kin groups. As a solitary god, Yahweh did not have to accord with such an ideal, and could all the more easily reach the status of sole God.

This elevation was made possible by the 'temporary exclusive worship' of oriental gods. A scene from the Akkadian Atrahasis epic will illustrate the nature of this institution. When a plague breaks out in the country it is attributed to the anger of the plague god Namtara. Therefore they decide to sacrifice only to Namtara for a time, and to neglect all other gods. This preferential treatment is enough to make the plague god change his mind. Because he is appeased he stops the plague. At another point in the same epic, the same treatment is given to Adad, the rain god, who restores his rain after a period of drought. If a god is accorded the special honour of 'provisional monolatry', then he or she has to accede to human wishes and help worshippers in their great need.

There are three clear examples of temporary monolatry in the Bible:

(*i*) Jeremiah 44:18: This text presupposes that only Yahweh was worshipped during the siege of Jerusalem, and that the cults of other deities were suspended.

(*ii*) Daniel 6: 8: The Persian King demands exclusive worship lasting thirty days.

(*iii*) Daniel 11:37–38: Here we are told of a king who orders all the gods to be neglected with the exception of a certain 'god of fortresses'—doubtless a war-god is intended.

It is worthy of note that temporary monolatry was also known among, and often practised by, pre-Islamic Arabs. It referred to the highest God of all, Allah. Mohammed repeatedly complained about this custom, for as soon as the petitioner was freed from his distress, he ended his exclusive worship of Allah (see, for instance, Sura 31:31–32, which mentions distress at sea and being brought safe to land). That was tantamount to a temporary orthodoxy, which could only make the prophet angry.

If we look at the history of the Yahweh-alone movement in connection with the political history of Israel, the notion of temporary monolatry can be offered as an explanation. We have to consider the distribution of political power. From the ninth century the two small kingdoms of Israel and Judah increasingly entered the sphere of influence of the near-Eastern powers. Both countries became subject to tribute and dependent on Assyria. In 722 the northern kingdom was downgraded to become an Assyrian province, and after 586 the southern kingdom also became an administrative district. During this continuously critical period a tendency became vocal which I have called the Yahweh-alone movement. It demanded the exclusive worship of the national deity. Only he who was concerned with the well-being of the State could be expected to help. When Judah as a State was crushed by the power of Babylon, the idea arose of a unique God who ruled the whole world. Accordingly monotheism is a reaction to a political crisis, one in which nothing can be expected of diplomacy and foreign military aid any longer. There is only one saviour: the one God. The history of the rise of monotheism is part of a broader history: that of the destruction of a small State.

Clearly monotheism as a *doctrine* could not solve Israel's political problems. But even when the doctrinal aspect of monotheism is stressed, Yahweh-alone supporters and early Jewish monotheists were not interested in dogma. That developed only with the Fathers of the Church and the scholastic theologians with their primarily speculative concerns. The theology of the Yahweh-alone movement is a theology of hope; one which wagers everything on *one* person, on Yahweh. Everything is hoped of him. Hosea and Deutero-Isaiah emphasise it: there is no god other than Yahweh who will act as a saviour (Hos. 13:14; Isa. 45:21). In theological jargon we might put it thus: soteriological monotheism is older than dogmatic monotheism. Or: hope is older and more original than belief.

Translated by J. G. Cumming

Notes

1. For evidence, see my articles: (*a*) 'Vor einer Wende im Verständnis des israelitschen Gottesglaubens?' in *Wie wird man Prophet in Israel?* (Düsseldorf 1980)

pp. 149–161 = *Theologische Quartalschrift* 160 (1980) 53–60; (*b*) 'Die Jahwe-allein-Bewegung', in: *Der einzige Gott: Die Geburt des biblischen Monotheismus* ed. B. Lang (Munich 1980) pp. 47–83 = *Monotheism and the Prophetic Minority. An Essay in Biblical History and Sociology* (Sheffield 1983) pp. 13–59; (*c*) 'Ein babylonisches Motiv in Israels Schöpfungsmythologie (Jer. 27:5–6)': *Biblische Zeitschrift* 27 (1983) 236–237.

2. In inscriptions from Hirbert el-Qom and Kuntillet Arud, Asherah seems to be named as the bride of Yahweh, but this appears to be an incorrect reading. We do not know the purport of the goddess Anath-Yahu in papyri of the Jewish colony on the island of Elephantine, or her relationship to Yahweh. Wisdom personified is not an actual but a poetical daughter of Yahweh (Prov. 8); originally she was doubtless an actual daughter of the creator god El, who in Ugaritic is additionally known as 'the wise'.

3. The worshipper of the Ugaritic god El is immediately connected with the 'sons of El' and Ashirat, the consort of El; see *Near Eastern Religious Texts Relating to the Old Testament* ed. W. Beyerlin (London and Philadelphia 1978), Ugaritic text No. 19.

Jürgen Moltmann

The Inviting Unity of the Triune God

1

IS CHRISTIANITY 'a monotheistic form of belief' (Schleiermacher)[1] and indeed as a monotheistic revealed religion 'the absolute religion' (Hegel)[2]? It is advisable to begin by taking a critical look at this way in which it has become usual of recent times in Europe to characterise Christianity and relate it to the history of religion in general. Monotheism has of course got a very long history and means the worship of the one unique God. But the modern European concept was presumably first introduced by Henry More and David Hume.[3] It did not denote the specifically Jewish belief. It expressed belief in progress and claimed superiority: Lessing's 'Education of the Human Race' goes from polytheism by way of pantheism to 'monotheism'. Hegel's step-by-step development of consciousness leads from natural religion by way of cultural religion to revealed religion. Pagan 'polytheism' is thus down-graded to be classed as 'primitive religion' and 'pantheism' as a religion of the emotions is given a lower rank than rational monotheism. The classification of religions indicated by the concept 'monotheism' is in its innocent form the naive absolutism of one's own religious perspective, but in its developed form nothing other than religious imperialism aimed at subjecting 'underdeveloped' peoples by liquidating their religions.

Before Christianity is formally classified as a 'monotheistic' religion, the contemporary criticism of monotheism needs to be taken seriously:

(*a*) Monotheism is not only the worship of a single unique God but also always the recognition of this God's single and unique universal monarchy. There is no monotheism without theocracy. The religions described as 'monotheistic'—Judaism, Christianity and Islam—are theocratic ways of perceiving life and the world. From the other side imperialistic world-conquerors have always tried to find a monotheistic and theocratic basis to legitimise their claims to domination. Hence the Mongol ruler Genghis Khan declared: 'In heaven there is no-one but the one God alone; on earth no-one but the one ruler Genghis Khan, the son of God.'[4]

(b) In the face of the one ruler of the universe in heaven there is for men and women only the attitude of subjection, not that of their own freedom. It can therefore be understood that of recent times in Europe Christian monotheism has called forth atheism as its one alternative: 'Either there is a God, and then man is not free; or man is free, and then there is no God.'[5] If religious monotheism is combined with absolutism at the level of both Church and State, then only atheism can rescue and safeguard freedom.

(c) Everywhere monotheism is recognisably the religion of patriarchal society: the rule of the Father of all heaven is mirrored by the rule of the father in the family. From this follow the disenfranchisment and enslavement of women. 'Monotheism' is only the religious summit of a religious order of domination that forces foreign peoples, women and nature into subjection and dependence.

(d) What from a 'monotheistic' point of view is termed 'polytheism' and 'natural religion' is in reality better understood as *spiritism*. It is a highly complex religious system that balances natural and supernatural powers. In shamanism, in the cosmic mysticism of China and in Hinduism are to be found the treasures of ancient ecological wisdom. In contrast to this monotheism's domination and exploitation of nature must be labelled primitive. Even in those polytheistic religions that derive their life from a pantheistic foundation the maternal mystery of nature is preserved. From this point of view monotheism with its masculine bias can hardly be regarded as a higher religious or even moral development for mankind.

If the Christian belief in God is not to share the distress of monotheism and be destroyed, then the unity of the triune God should no longer simply be termed 'monotheistic' but should be more precisely defined with reference to the freedom of men and women, the peace of nations, and the presence of the spirit in all natural things.

2

Ancient Israel is usually made responsible for the emergence and formation of strict monotheism. But with reference to the modern concept of 'monotheism' this is not correct. What people have said since the Enlightenment is that Israel was the first to overcome polytheism and introduce the ethical worship of one God. Israel was the first nation to understand its national divine father as the 'united God' and thus lay the foundation for religious universalism. The *shema Yisrael* still sounds today like the original form of monotheism: 'Hear, O Israel: The Lord our God is one Lord; and you shall love the Lord your God with all your heart, and with all your soul, and with all your might' (Deut. 6:4–5). It could be said that polytheism scatters people's attention among many different gods and powers, whereas this Jewish monotheism concentrates it on the one God and thus focuses man on a person. The powers of nature then lose their divinity and are seen as merely earthly natural powers. Acknowledgment of the transcendent God makes the immanent world the profane world of mankind.

But if one looks more closely at this confession of Israel one discovers that God is acknowledged not as 'One God' but as 'One Lord'. As the first commandment shows, his dominion is concerned with the liberation of the people from servitude in Egypt to life in freedom in alliance with this God. What is acknowledged is not the one God's transcendence of this world but the act of liberation immanent in the world on the part of the unique Lord. The exodus from slavery is the one reason for having 'no other gods beside him', as the second commandment states. Because the experience of the exodus was constitutive for Israel and is re-enacted at every Passover, the acknowledgment of the Lord is exclusive. It does not suffer any other Lord besides. But this does not mean that this God must in himself be a numerical or monadic unity. On the contrary: the God of the Exodus and of the Covenant is at one and the same time transcendent and immanent with regard to the world. He has nothing to do with the metaphysical one that stands in opposition to the physical many. Nor has he anything to do with that moral transcendence that is contrasted with man's immanent fulfilment of his duty as a source of responsibility. Rather, he dwells among the people he has chosen. Hence recent Jewish thinkers have corrected the Enlightenment thesis of 'Mosaic monotheism' and presented a more differentiated picture of the unity of the God of Israel.

This is how Franz Rosenzweig interprets the *shema Yisrael*: 'The *shekinah*, God's settlement and dwelling among men, is thought of as a division that takes place within God himself. God himself divides himself from himself, he gives himself away to his people, he shares in suffering its sufferings, he goes with it into the misery of exile, he shares in its wanderings. . .' In this surrender by God of himself to Israel there is 'a divine suffering'. God, who 'shares in suffering' Israel's fate, makes himself 'in need of redemption'. If Israel's sufferings are overcome, then God's suffering with Israel ceases. If Israel attains its freedom, then the God dwelling in Israel attains his blessedness, in other words himself. The division in God is overcome and transcended. Then

God will be *one* God. This reunion of God's *shekinah* dwelling in Israel with God himself is anticipated in every acknowledgement of God as the 'one Lord'. 'Acknowledging God's unity—the Jew calls this uniting God. For this unity exists to the extent that it comes into being, it is unity in formation. And this becoming is entrusted to man's soul and hands.[6]

The God of the Exodus, the God who dwells among the people of his Covenant, is a God who differentiates himself and identifies himself with himself. In this process of differentiation his 'unity' is not an exclusive but an inclusive unity, in other words a unity uniting Israel with itself. Prayer and acknowledgment of the one Lord must therefore be conceived and used as active factors of this divine unity that unites with God.

Abraham Heschel, too, has clearly distinguished Israel's history of God from metaphysical and political monotheism.[7] His starting-point is not the sovereign impassibility of the ruler of the world but the passionate feeling of the God of Israel. In his creative emotion with its readiness to suffer, God goes out of himself and enters into his creation. He becomes the companion in suffering of his people. He dwells in heaven and at the same time with the poor and those without rights. Heschel thus presents the God of Israel as a 'bipolar God' and uses for this the idea of the sprit of God (*ruah*) who renews the face of the earth (Psalm 104:30) and creates for man a pure heart and a new spirit (Psalm 51:10). It is in his creative emotion that God's inner differentiations arise: as creator he continues to transcend the world, but in his spirit he is involved in his creation and 'is in all things' (Wisdom 12:1). Even more important is the way God distinguishes and reveals himself in his name 'Lord': compare Exodus 6:3 and Isaiah 51:15 with 1 Cor. 8:6: 'Yet for us there is one God, the Father, . . . and one Lord, Jesus Christ.' One cannot therefore define God's unity exclusively by means of elimination and delimination in such a way that what is ultimately indivisible counts as the one that defines everything, but it must be understood as a unity that differentiates itself, goes out from itself, invites the other to join it and unites it with itself.

3

On the basis of the history of God to which the New Testament bears witness, Christianity is indeed the *Trinitarian* confession of the Father, the son and the Holy Spirit. But in its own history, especially in the West, it has given a one-sided emphasis to the unity of the triune God. In its arguments against the polytheism of the various nations Christianity presented itself as the superior universal religion of the one God.[8] When Christianity became involved with the Roman empire and seized the opportunity to become the imperial religion, it placed the universal monarchy of the one God in the foreground, and from this the Christian emperor could derive the legitimation of his sovereignty and the multinational Christian imperium its inner unity. While the Nicene creed of 325 still described the unity of the Son with the Father as a unity of substance, *homoousios*, and thus stressed the hypostatic difference between the Father and the Son, the Athanasian creed, of Western origin, already put in the foreground the thesis 'God is one'. God's unity thus does not merely consist in the united divine substance of the Father, the Son and the Spirit, but in the one identical divine subjectivity in which he acts externally. Augustine's famous distinction between God's works needing to be inwardly divided but externally undivided (*ad intra divisa, ad extra indivisa*) has given rise to the idea that the triune God may within himself be differentiated in a trinitarian way but that he appears to the outside world monotheistically as one in action and manifestation. The doctrine of the trinity is in this case nothing other than 'Christian monotheism'.[9] But if one calls the Christian acknowledgment of God 'trinitarian monotheism' then one clings firmly to the pyramidal structure of monotheism and only introduces a trinitarian differentiation at the very top.

The unity of the triune God is then seen in the monarchy of God. This was admittedly stressed by the Greek Fathers too, but they did not equate the nature of the triune God with his lordship over the world, for the latter consisted in the economy of salvation, while it was the doxology that first acknowledged and praised the eternal nature of the triune God. But in the West the essential unity of the triune God was seen in his lordship and equated with it. God is one, that is, he is one lord, one person, one subject, one divine I—this was still Karl Barth's interpretation.[10] If this is the right starting point, then the three divine persons of the Father, the Son and the Spirit can only be seen as modes of being 'in' which the one God exists. The unity of the triune God then resides in the sovereignty of his lordship. Therefore the root of the doctrine of the trinity is to be found in the proposition 'God reveals himself as the Lord'.[11]

But this monotheistic proposition does not appear in the New Testament in this form. According to the New Testament's professions of faith Jesus is the Lord and God is the Father of our Lord Jesus Christ (Rom. 15:6; 1 Cor. 1:3; 2 Cor. 11:31; Eph. 3:14; etc.). All the New Testament's professions of faith start from the trinitarian difference between God the Father of Jesus and Jesus the Lord. The Father who out of unconditional love sends his own son Jesus and sacrifices him for the redemption of the world has raised him up from the dead and established him as Lord of his kingdom. The Son will exercise his liberating and redeeming lordship (Rom. 14:8–9) until the final consummation and will then hand the kingdom over to the Father (1

Cor. 15:24). The trinitarian difference between God the Father and the Lord Jesus Christ opens up the history of salvation and is directed at that perfect union of which it can be said that in it 'God is all in all' (1 Cor. 15:28). Without this trinitarian difference between God the Father and the Lord Jesus Christ the history of salvation cannot be understood as the taking up of all creation into the redeeming community of God.

At least since the start of the Romanisation of Christianity there has been an equation of 'Father' and 'Lord' in the concept of God—an equation with serious consequences. According to Lactantius the one God is Lord and Father at one and the same time: 'We must all love him, because he is the Father, but also fear him, because he is the Lord.'[12] The double structure of fearing and loving God corresponds to the 'two persons' in God, his role as Lord and as Father. Men and women are therefore always God's servants and children at one and the same time. This Romanisation of the image of God also involved transferring the Roman *patria potestas* to God: God holds the *potestas vitae necisque*, the power of life and death. Once masculine domination in the family, in the State and in the Church was legitimised by this image of God, monarchical forms of lordship arose. According to whether there was more emphasis on God's role as father or on his role as lord there was more emphasis on the political patriarchalism of the 'Father of the Country' or the political absolution of the ruler. But in this dominant Father of All we can no longer recognise the Father of Jesus Christ whom Jesus himself addressed so trustingly and tenderly as *Abba*. In the father-like Lord of Heaven we can no longer find Jesus, 'the friend of publicans and sinners'.[13]

If we wish to return from these historical deformations of the Christian image of God to the original biblical confession of faith, then we must define the unity of the triune God not in a monotheistic but in a trinitarian way. The history of Jesus with the God whom he called 'my father' in the Spirit that was experienced as the Holy Spirit—the history to which the New Testament bears witness—is a history that takes place between different subjects, as is shown by the story of Gethsemane. Father, Son and Spirit are distinct subjects with will and reason who communicate with each other in prayer and response, are turned towards each other in love, and are only 'one' together. While Paul and the synoptics mean by God the Father of Jesus Christ and clearly subordinate Jesus the Son, in St John's gospel we find a developed trinitarian language: 'I and the Father are one,' says the Johannine Jesus. He distinguishes between 'I' and 'you' and points to a unity which is to be found not only in mutual recognition and shared will but also in mutual indwelling: 'I am in the Father and the Father in me' (John 14:11, 17:21, and elsewhere). With the Father the Son may not form a single entity but he is one with him, which is expressed by means of the plural 'we' and 'us'. If one wishes to translate this intimate and unique unity of the Father and the Son into trinitarian terms, then the best means is the concept of perichoresis. The divine persons exist not only with and for each other but also *in each other*: the Son in the Father, the Father in the Son, the Spirit in the Father and in the Son. Thanks to their eternal love the divine persons exist so intimately in each other that they constitute themselves in their unique, incomparable and perfect unity. This perichoretic concept of the unity of the triune God is the trinitarian concept of unity. It should be noted that this trinitarian unity is to be grasped equally originally with the persons of the trinity. Their unity is not a secondary 'community' of the persons, nor are the persons secondary 'modes of being' of the one God. The perichoretic concept of the unity of the trinity links God's threeness and oneness together without reducing the one to the other. The dangers of modalism and of tritheism are equally excluded.

If we can best grasp the biblically attested history of the Father, the Son and the Spirit with the concept of perichoresis, then the concept of the unity of the triune God needs to be developed not only in a trinitarian but also in a soteriological manner. It is precisely this that is expressed by the 'high-priestly prayer' of the Johannine Jesus: 'That they may all be one; even as thou, Father, art in me, and I in thee, that they also may be in us, so that the world may believe that thou hast sent me' (John 17:21). The community of Jesus's friends is meant to correspond to the perichoretic community of the Father and the Son. It is not the persons of the trinity and their relations but their perichoretic community that has its effect and is reproduced in the community of Jesus. But this community does not only correspond to the triune God but also exists 'in him' by the power of the Holy Spirit. The perichoretic unity of the triune God is therefore an open, inviting unity that unites with itself. It is not confined to God in order to define him exclusively as the one over against the many, but is inclusively open for all creation, whose misery consists in isolation from the living God and whose salvation is thus to be found in being graciously taken up into the community of God. The perichoretic concept of the unity of the Father, the Son and the Holy Spirit would not correspond to the history of salvation attested in the Bible if it were not understood soteriologically as an integrative concept of unity. Because of the gracious love that flows out in abundance the trinity is 'open' to those who are lost. It is open for all created beings who are loved, found and accepted. The triune God does not stand transcendentally outside the world. 'It is far better to say that the relationship of the divine persons to each other is so wide that the entire world finds room there.'[14]

The Christian acknowledgment of the triune God is originally a baptismal confession of faith. It expresses and constitutes the community of the triune God. It is the new community of human beings, Jews or pagans, Greeks or barbarians, lords or slaves, men and women in Christ (Rom. 10:12, Gal. 3:28), a community in which they are 'of one heart and soul' and 'have everything in common' so that 'there is not a needy person among them' (Acts 4:32–34). That is the life of the trinity and the inviting picture of the triune God on earth.

4

As opposed to the deformations of life by monotheism which were mentioned at the start and which have rightly been criticised, trinitarian belief and the inviting trinitarian life of love press for the following changes:

(a) The one-sided patterns of domination and subjection are replaced by forms of community based on free agreement. At the grass-roots the Church consists of and in such communities and exists through them. This also means the democratisation of the process of decision in political and economic life. It can also lead to the decentralisation of political and economic power, to the extent that better systems of communication are built up to link togther into a single network the individual communities in which one can keep track of what is going on.

(b) Man's patriarchal privileges and the deformation of woman they bring about are overcome. The trinitarian community is a community of brothers and sisters and can become the model of a human community.

(c) The trinitarian community is experienced in the Holy Spirit. The fellowship of the Holy Spirit binds men and women together. The Spirit is thus also easily called the communal spirit or the communal divinity. But the community of the spirit does not only embrace man's liberation and redemption but from the start determines the community of creation (Psalm 104). By means of the indwelling spirit of creation all creatures are related to each other in such a way that they exist for each other, with each other, and in each other. The mystery of creation is the perichoresis of creatures in the indwelling of the divine spirit. A universal cosmic 'sympathy' keeps creation alive. 'Thou sparest all things, for they are thine, O Lord who lovest the living. For thy immortal spirit is in all things' (Wisdom 11:26–12:1). The trinitarian confession of faith leads to the discovery of God's spirit in all things and the life of the trinity leads men and women back into the community of creation, since from being the masters and exploiters of nature they become once again members of that all-embracing community.

If we bring these remarks togther we can finally understand the Christian doctrine of the trinity as a critical counterbalance and apply it as follows:

(a) By the link between God the Father and the fate of Jesus monarchical patriarchalism has been made impossible. God the Father is Jesus' 'Abba', and only he who sees this son sees the Father.

(b) By the link between Jesus, the Son of Man, and God, whom he called 'Abba', his dear Father, that atheistic humanism is made impossible that offers the man Jesus sympathy but rejects every God, including Jesus' God.

(c) By the link between the Spirit and the Father of Jesus Christ as well as with the figure of the Son polytheistic spiritism is made impossible—the outlook that sees many spirits in nature and values them according to their power.

But by means of the doctrine of the trinity the elements of truth are in this way set free and united in the religion of the Father, in the religion of the Son and in the religion of the Spirit.

Translated by Robert Nowell

Notes:

1. F. Schleiermacher *Glaubenslehre*, 2nd edition, § 11.
2. G. W. F. Hegel *Philosophie der Religion*, part 3.
3. See *Historisches Wörterbuch der Philosophie* s.v. 'Monotheismus', vol. VI pp. 142–146.
4. M. de Ferdinandy *Tschingis Khan* (Hamburg 1958) p. 153.
5. Jean-Paul Sartre *Ist der Existentialismus ein Humanismus?* (1946).
6. F. Rosenzweig *Der Stern der Erlösung* (Heidelberg 1954) part 3, book 2, pp. 192 ff. See also S. Ben-Chorin *Jüdischer Glaube* (Tübingen 1975) 1: 'Monotheismus als Ausschliesslichkeit Gottes', pp. 31 ff.
7. A. Heschel *The Prophets* (New York 1962) pp. 252 ff.
8. For a more detailed treatment of this point see J. Moltmann *The Trinity of the Kingdom of God* (London 1981).
9. Karl Barth *Kirchliche Dogmatik* I/1 (Zürich 1932) pp. 371, 374.
10. *Ibid.* pp. 368 ff.
11. *Ibid.* pp. 320 ff.
12. Lactantius *Vom Zorne Gottes* (*De ira Dei*), edited by H. Kraft and A. Wlosok (Darmstadt 1974) p. 77.
13. J. Moltmann 'Ich glaube an Gott den Vater. Patriarchalische oder nicht-patriarchalische Rede von Gott?', in *Evangelische Theologie* 43 (1983) 397 ff. In this article I have presented the historical connections in greater detail.
14. Adrienne von Speyr quoted by B. Albrecht *Eine Theologie des Katholischen. Einführung in das Werk Adrienne von Speyrs* (Einsiedeln 1973) I p. 126.

Christian Duquoc

Monotheism and Unitary Ideology

ERIK PETERSON'S work on 'monotheism as a political problem' (in *Theologische Traktate*, Munich, 1951, pp. 45–149) has cast a certain suspicion on monotheism's interests and function and on what is at stake in it. More recently in France, the writers known as neo-pagans, with Alain de Benoist (*Comment peut-on être païen*, Paris, 1981) as their leader, have taken up vigorously the criticism of monotheism's social and political functions. What is involved is Christian monotheism: if I am to believe the preface with which M. Augé begins his work *Le Génie du paganisme* (Paris, 1982, pp. 15–16), the chief reproach brought against it is of having destroyed the present for the benefit of the future. But M. Augé adds, with bitterness or subtlety: 'What would be the use of overcoming history at the price of the present? If it is true that a god ought to bring men happiness on earth, this should be tomorrow . . . Which is the more illusory: to want everything all at once or to wait for nothing but history, that is to say, for someone who is living, death?'

This suspicion about the vicious effects of monotheism reaches its full expansion in the comfort which it is supposed to bring to policies of intolerance by enveloping them with the aura of the sacred. In paganism, the divine represented a form of appreciation of the vitality and sacredness of the universe. It is also essentially plural in its manifestation and tolerant in its demands; effervescent and whimsical like nature; inspiring with enthusiasm and festive; welcoming and not fanatical; and ultimately non-violent, because it sustains all the possible differences. New gods come to be born without the old ones taking offence thereby. There is nothing of this with the monotheism that emerges from the Bible: one is dealing with a jealous God. You are to have no other God but him: the assembly of the gods is dissolved, and those

59

who would be minded to serve their images would be annihilated. Tolerance is regarded as an erroneous laxity. Phinehas was praised for ever for having put idolaters to the sword. Biblical monotheism is thus from the start partly linked with intransigence and intolerance. This was well understood by the civilization of antiquity with its tolerance of different religions: monotheism represented a danger for the Greek or Roman way of life; it introduced fanaticism where there prevailed mutual respect and amused recognition. The reaction of persecution was from one point of view an act of self-defence: in Christianity the pagans saw a threat to their ideals and their customs. The way in which Christians worshipped their God by excluding all the others made one think that this intolerance would bring forth bitter fruit socially and politically. Once the Empire was converted, the laws restricting paganism and the destruction of pagan temples would bear witness to the pagans' perspicacity: the monotheism that came forth from the Judaeo-Christian tradition is of such a nature that it does not acknowledge any place for any other form of the divine, nor finally for any other form of ethics other than that which it decrees. Hence the unitary ideology with which the Catholic Church is thought to be infected is seen as being immanent in the very way in which Christian monotheism is and was affirmed. The aim of this article is to explore the truth or falsity of this judgement. To do this, I shall begin by evoking the ambiguous function of monotheism in the Christian scheme of things; I shall then discuss the foundation of the unitary ideology in Catholicism; and I shall conclude by suggesting some conditions for transcending this ideology.

1. THE AMBIGUITY OF MONOTHEISM

Blaming monotheism for the Catholic unitary ideology and its most visible consequence, intolerance, cannot be based on the following kind of deductive reasoning: If God is one, he demands a unique social form of acknowledging him. Every attempt at escaping this imperative would meet with sanctions: it would indeed be up to the group bearing witness to this truth to establish it in the political, cultural and social worlds. Christianity's idea of making all men brothers on the basis of a juridical, cultural and ecclesial unity had its roots in the acknowledgment of a single God, Father of all men, the giver of their salvation and the punisher of their misdeeds. In a word, the deduction seemed faultless: corresponding to acknowledgement of a single God was the wish by the group bearing witness to him for unitary rule, not out of a thirst for power but out of a sense of duty, since outside this bond with the one God men would be lost. The unpopularity caused by intolerance was preferable to the populist laxity leading to perdition.

In fact, this reasoning is too abstract to explain what actually happened in history. All monotheisms are not totalitarian and intolerant: Hellenistic monotheism was not, and in many primitive religions where the supreme form of God is acknowledged there does not exist any intolerance. Although it may be hazardous to apply the term monotheism to Hinduism, it is not entirely out of place, and it does not seem that Hinduism drives people to intolerance: it is possible for it to welcome Christian monotheism, but the reverse is not in fact true. These few examples taken from outside the biblical field provoke one into suspecting the ideological character of monotheism's involvement: what is accused is one form of monotheism as it was understood by certain Christian groups. These attributed a function to it which it does not possess of its own account because it does not always produce the same effects. An example drawn from our own history shows us that this is so: the philosophy of the Enlightenment fought for tolerance. Everyone recalls the Calas affair because of Voltaire's intervention. But intervening on behalf of tolerance did not mean for him an avowal of atheism: on the contrary. It was not in monotheism that the philosophers of the Enlightenment saw the seeds of intolerance but in the positive historic religion represented by Christianity. Through its belief that God had endorsed a particular history—that of the Jews to start with by their election, that of Jesus through his sonship, and that of the Church by the gift of the Spirit—this turned particularities into absolutes in what is termed an example of positivity and excluded all other possible forms of relationship to God. It is not without significance that we had to wait for Vatican II to ratify the idea and the practice of religious freedom or to acknowledge the positive value of other religions. God's endorsement of a particular history thus led to intolerance and to a unitary ideology: one God, one faith, one baptism, one Lord Jesus Christ drove one to acknowledge only one authentic actual Church. What governs the matter is not the fact of one God but of one historic Lord who brings into operation the process of the historicity of the Church's witness and thus of the particular sign of membership, of which the opposite is exclusion. This is true of baptism, as it was of circumcision. The struggle of the philosophers of the Enlightenment, too, was waged against the particularist and exclusive implications of God's involvement in history. God is made manifest by all cosmic or human phenomena, but not by taking sides in social conflicts. That kind of God raises to universal significance an attitude which, by being made divine, devalues every other individual form in history. The philosophers of the Enlightenment played the one and universal God off against his biblical and Christian particularisation.

A second, contemporary test can be applied to this stand by the philosophy of the Enlightenment. Two works have appeared in France recently, one by G. Morel (*Questions d'homme*, three volumes, Paris, 1977), the other by B. H. Lévy (*Le Testament de Dieu*, Paris, 1979), which accord monotheism a liberating function.

In the case of G. Morel it is not a question of recapitulating the tradition of the Enlightenment, which is too aridly rationalist, but of a dialectic between reason and mysticism. This gives a surprising strength to his argument for the gratuitousness of contact with God. This God is close to everyone, and that is why he does not become involved in history: to become involved in history is to choose, and to choose is to exclude ('I have loved Jacob but I have hated Esau'). Forming an alliance means rejecting at the same time: the liberation of the Hebrews from Egypt was balanced by the death of the innocent first-born of the Egyptians. To de-historicise God is not to make him abstract but to recognise that he is close to everyone. It is to place history in the truth that it is provisional; it is to refuse to make it divine on the pretext that it would be a 'mechanism for making gods'. Following a line of thought very different from the interests of the philosophy of the Enlightenment, G. Morel makes monotheism perform an analogous function with regard to positive or historical religions: it shatters intolerance on the basis of the gratuitousness of every contact with the divine. The divinisation of history leads to the unitary ideology.

The other writer I have mentioned is working within a different framework but reaches similar conclusions. He is concerned to analyse the Marxist interpretation of history and the flexibility of law that this gives rise to. Briefly, Marxist totalitarianism, by virtue of its infallible scientific analysis of social relationships and by virtue of its utopia of a history without conflicts, re-shapes this in function of the end that is hoped for. The result is clear, and it can be verified in a good many countries which have chosen this option: outside the dialectic of history, of which the Communist parties are the authentic interpreters, all that exists is aberration. Faced with this doctrinal, social, cultural, juridical and political intolerance, B. H. Lévy recalls the Jewish doctrine not of God's involvement in history but of his irrevocable promise: law has nothing to do with necessity and the majority. It is because this promise is not historical, because it is not conditioned by history, that it relativises all history and demolishes all totalitarianism. The function of monotheism is once more both to prevent the erection of a system and to prevent the primacy of force or success over law. Here again, whatever one may think of B. H. Lévy's monotheism, one cannot deny the rigour of his argumentation and the liberating function which he acknowledges in monotheism in virtue of its essential distance from history. This is not without significance in someone who appeals to the Jewish tradition.

The attempts made since the age of the Enlightenment to exorcise monotheism of its intolerance of the positive religions indicate the abstract character of the judgments that see in it a major source of the unitary ideology.

2. THE BASIS OF THE UNITARY IDEOLOGY

'One God, one faith, one baptism, one Lord,' one Catholic Church, the latter being the place where the different levels of unity find concrete expression: this is how one would express the hierarchical series on which the Catholic unitary ideology is based. It would be wrong to say that the first member of the series could be isolated from the whole of the sequence. Our brief excursus into history and philosophy has confirmed that monotheism has played an ambiguous role and thus that it cannot on its own be the basis for the Catholic Church's unitary ideology. This basis is historical or positive: it is not transcendant. I would like to say that it is the way in which the Church makes God act historically that leads monotheism to play the ideological role of providing the foundation for a practice of uniformity. What is involved is a deflection of the aim of monotheism. The Catholic Church acknowledges that in Jesus Christ God has become definitively involved with our history. God has thus chosen one precise road for reaching us. This road is represented by the life of the Galilean which finds its culmination in the defeat of the cross that is then given a positive endorsement in the Resurrection. This road cannot be by-passed: scripture makes it universal, and the Church bears witness to its definitive character.

The Church is in fact limited and defined by this road: it is not something it makes up, but is mapped out in our history as the particular history to which the Church ascribes the value of universal mediation. By virtue of its witness with regard to the one road open in our history the Church is thus the only place of salvation: without baptism and the faith received and acknowledged in its bosom, salvation is excluded. The old saying 'No salvation outside the Church' transcribed the conviction of the uniqueness of this road. What we are talking about when we say 'Church' is a particular group that can be identified, that has been established, that has been affected by a multitude of experiences, that is bound and liberated by its history or its memory. The particularity of the Catholic Church prolongs the particularity of its origin. Being particular is to mark oneself off from other groups by one's customs, one's laws, one's habits, one's beliefs. Identifying the Catholic group historically is simple. To be recognised, whether extended through time or extended through space, it needs symbolic signs: creeds, rites, doctrines, customs, hierarchical organisation, etc. Episcopal collegiality with its links to the Roman primacy sustains Catholic unity as an original historical phenomenon.

Here we are at the level of practice, which in itself would not be enough: it needs to have attributed to it a doctrinal justification and some would say an ideological one. Its coherence exists at the symbolic and practical level: otherwise the group would become diluted and would not be able to hold together populations of such diverse ethnic and cultural origins. The historical and empirical character of the group which bears witness to the original road followed by Jesus forces it to create symbolic signs of mutual recognition and to institutionalise its hierarchical organisation, its rituals and its beliefs in order to face the challenge of the times and of the variety of civilisations. The basis for the Catholic Church's unitary ideology is its desire for universalism without abandoning its own identity: it is only as a side-effect or as a second-order act that it will refer to a historically-oriented monotheism in order to explain its uniformity in practice and indeed for its Roman centralisation. In my view monotheism only plays a secondary role in the establishment of the unitary ideology. Of course, it provides a justification, but precisely because it is accepted as a principle of ideological utility and not as a questioning transcendant force. The transcendance that is alleged for this basis is illusory, for in reality it is historical and contingent: monotheism, by means of its biblical originality of historical involvement, serves to establish the worth of the group bearing witness to God. What is involved here is a perversion: the aim of election was not the exaltation of Israel and the immutability of its laws but the witness borne to the living God. I would also like before concluding to underline the destabilising and not justificatory character of Christian monotheism.

3. TRANSCENDING THE UNITARY IDEOLOGY

Ideology is the intellectualisation of a particular dominant practice. Monotheism has played this role, but it is not its foundation. This ideology is linked to the logic of Christianity's positive nature as the absolute road of encounter with God. But it is not easy to maintain the divergence between the historically established unitary practice of Catholicism and its alleged basis, monotheism. The philosophy of the Enlightenment and G. Morel's recent effort had to reject the incarnation of the Son of God in order to purge monotheism of compromise with intolerance. As these thinkers saw very clearly, fanaticism and the unitary ideology have their origin in the divinisation of a particular being, thus turning into an absolute a contingent form of what is always a multiform relationship with God and excluding all other forms. On this interpretation the incarnation establishes an indestructible link between this road, eliminating every other road from now on, and God's decision to reveal himself and to be recognised by this road alone. Without the incarnation several roads would theoretically remain possible and hence tolerance would be obligatory, since God would not himself have turned any form of acknowledging him into an absolute. We are thus apparently faced with a dilemma: either to free God of his historical burden by denying the incarnation and restoring to monotheism its questioning power with regard to all forms claiming to provide access to the transcendant, or to link God radically to this history and this Church to the exclusion of all others by means of his indestructible bond with the man Jesus acknowledged as God and Son, and thus to enter upon ideology and favour intolerance. A dilemma forces one to choose: the philosophy of the Enlightenment and G. Morel have opted for the first born of the dilemma. We see that the official Catholic Church in the nineteenth century opposed any nibbling away of its universality and condemned religious freedom. The Second Vatican Council has balanced this stand by favouring a position which would neither be the unacceptable one of breaking with the Church's tradition of acknowledging Jesus as Son of God nor the too radical position of the Enlightenment.

Is this new orientation simply a question of emotion and tactics? Is it possible to hold it within the framework of monotheism with a historical and therefore contingent manifestation? The criticisms offered by someone like G. Morel show that the effort undertaken to get out of this dilemma is not self-evident. Nevertheless it seems to me that monotheism in its historical Christian form offers an opportunity for this new way of locating the Church with regard to freedom and with regard to other faiths. On this interpretation the unitary ideology would be an archaism, since universality would not have been able to have an established pattern. At all events, it would not be able to base itself on Christian monotheism.

Christian monotheism is in fact the outcome of the differences that are accepted and endorsed within the communion: we speak of the trinitarian image of God. The Father is not confounded with his Son Jesus, and the Spirit does not universalise merely the particularity of the man from Nazareth: it makes every new situation open to questioning by the message of the Gospel. It has not been given to close and to perpetuate but to open and to create. The differences expressed in this way do not replace each other, nor are they added to each other: they are expressed in a unity of communion that we acknowledge as God. This prevents us from identifying the series of divine actors with just one thread, that of the man from Nazareth. The Spirit bloweth where it listeth, and Jesus never claimed that it was only blowing in him. The gift of the Spirit does not make Jesus's particularity an absolute but locates it as the critical focus for the other roads of access to God. The difference of role of the divine actors in our history invites us to reject turning Jesus's road into an absolute: it does not exclude a historical legitimacy of other roads. As a result, the unitary ideology has an institutional and practical basis: it arises from the group's claim to justify imposing its truth but does not go back to monotheism acknowledged under the images of the Trinity.

Contrary to rumour, nothing is less certain than that monotheism sustains the Catholic Church's ideology of uniformity. Universalist practice and its hierarchical structure have in fact made monotheism play this role of ideological basis. But in doing this the Catholic Church has corrupted what it nevertheless does not cease to proclaim: that the God of Jesus Christ is the Father of all men, that he bestows the Spirit on whom he wills, and that no Church is able to particularise his action to the point of making it transparent in its history and in its structure. The invisibility of the Spirit and its openness to every man and woman attack every deductive form of ecclesiology. Accepting and endorsing precariousness, contingency and particularity was not for Jesus to make them absolute or divine, to fix them: it was to invite us to encounter God in what is intermediate and to urge us to reject the mystical dream or fusion. There is nothing there that makes for intolerance. On the contrary, the intercommunion of the divine actors with their different roles in history opens up a space which contradicts the closing in of the ideology of uniformity. The philosophy of the Enlightenment and G. Morel went too far in their criticisms of Christianity: they did not calculate that its own monotheistic confession of faith was the surest warrant of its temptation to uniformity.

Translated by Robert Nowell

Robert Caspar

The Permanent Significance of Islam's Monotheism

MONOTHEISM is the essential common feature of what are rightly called the three great monotheistic religions, Judaism, Christianity and Islam, though other religions share it to different extents. However, none of the three religions practises and defines it in the same way, and it has served in the past as a reason for polemics and even armed confrontations. The time has now come when difference can be experienced as enrichment, a mutual questioning to purify and deepen our own faith, to highlight what is really common to us all and where our fundamental differences lie, leading us towards the greatest possible degree of joint witness in our day to the one God.

1. ISLAM'S MONOTHEISM

Belief in the one transcendent God is undoubtedly the specific feature of Islam, in two senses. First, it distinguishes it from the other great monotheistic religions: 'If Israel is rooted in hope and Christianity vowed to charity, Islam is centred on faith.'[1] A recent study on monotheism preferred to regard Judaism as centred on the oneness of God's action rather than of his essence, around the notion of covenant and the choice of a people, and Christianity centred on the uniqueness of the mediation of Jesus Christ.[2] This author forgot the monotheism of Islam, a frequent occurrence. Islam's monotheism is a direct object of belief and doctrine, without chosen people or mediation, even if it recognises the action of God in human history through the prophets he sent and the interventions of his almighty power. This *dogmatic* character of

67

Moslem monotheism seems to me its specific feature.[3] Secondly, belief in the one transcendent God is the axis around which all Islam's doctrine and practice is organised. The whole Koran is nothing other than an urgent and reiterated repetition of that faith, of its history in humanity and its consequences in personal and social life. It could be called the one, sufficient dogma. The Moslem at the moment of death, however defective his or her faith or practice may have been, is assured of forgiveness and paradise by pronouncing the *shahâda*, the testimony to the monotheistic faith: 'There is no God but God.' For a person who can no longer say the words, it is enough to raise their index finger, or for someone to raise it for them. At least, this is the general opinion. We shall now give some details of this doctrine.

2. THE ONENESS OF GOD

God's oneness is defined in the Koran as a strict monotheism. The definition was used first against the polytheism of Arabia in the sixth to seventh centuries, which resembled that of the Canaanites described in the Bible,[4] with carved stone columns, one god per tribe, with one or two goddesses seated beside him (*sâhiba*, 'companion of the God', see Kor. 6, 101; 72.3), their coupling engendering other gods or heroes. The brief *sūra*, No 112, 'the *sūra* of the *tawhîd* (oneness of God)', which is constantly repeated, carved on mosques, decorates houses, is directed in the first place to these engenderings: 'Say: God is one, he is indissociable, he does not beget and he is not begotten.' It was only later that it was applied to the Christian ideas of divine fatherhood and sonship, understood in a carnal sense.

While at the beginning of the Koranic revelation there are traces of henotheism, indicated in the original sense of the famous Moslem warcry *Allâh akbar*, 'God is the greatest,' the Koran very soon denied any divinity 'beyond God' (*min dûn Allâh*, another frequently repeated formula). God is the sole creator and all other beings, from angel to clay, are his creatures, 'created to adore God'.

Numerous signs of this oneness are offered in the Koran. The earlier prophets said the same; the harmony of the world and of human beings is evidence of it. Finally, God has revealed in the Koran that he is one. To 'associate' creatures with God is the only unforgivable sin, *shirk*, infidelity. It is notable that the problem of the existence of God is touched on only indirectly, through that of the oneness, because it was hardly an issue. Later Moslem theology, which discourses at length on the proofs of God's oneness, treats the existence of God merely as one more of the many divine attributes, 'existent'. Moreover, many theologians, like the greatest, Ghazâlî (ninth century), regard both propositions as not worth wasting time on, so obvious are they: if God exists, he can only be one. This is inscribed in human nature; before birth every man or woman has professed the monotheistic faith in pre-eternity (Koran 7, 172–173). This 'covenant' between God and man, the substitute for the biblical covenant, concerns every human being, who is born 'naturally Moslem', as the famous *hadith* (saying of Mohammed) declares: 'Every newborn infant is born a Moslem monotheist;[5] it is parents who make children Jews, Christians or Mazdeans.'

3. THE TRANSCENDENCE OF GOD

This one God is transcendent, in the exact sense of the term. He is the totally other and 'nothing is like him' (Kor. 112, 4; but see also 42, 11, etc.). The idea of creation introduces a radical division between the creator and creatures, in contrast to religions based on emanation or mystical experience. Nevertheless it must be stressed that transcendence does not mean distance. 'The remote God of Islam' is no less nonsense for being so often repeated. God is close to man, and invites each person to come close to him (Koran). This mutual closeness (*qurb*) is in fact the idea which best defines the relations of God and human beings, even at the summit of the orthodox mystical journey (Ghazâlî). No-one with any experience of the ordinary lives of Moslems could fail to feel this presence of God, not simply in his action, which tends to be an invasion, but through his being and his relation to the believer.

This transcendence is emphasised particularly by the rejection of any intermediary, of any mediation other than the Koran between God and human beings. While the Koran seems to accept some cases of intercession (the angels, the Prophet), both ancient and modern Islam make a boast of this rejection: no mediation, still less if there is question of an incarnate God, no Church, no sacraments; an extremely sober liturgy in bare mosques, where the believer is alone before God, even at the Friday common prayer. True, popular religion, in Islam as elsewhere, has always tried to fill this void. The religious brotherhoods have multiplied the lines of holiness and, for most people in both town and country, religion consists above all in invoking the local saint and visiting his 'marabout'. However, all Islamic reform movements for centuries have had as their chief aim the suppression of these 'reprehensible innovations' (*bida*'). This phenomenon reveals both Islam as it wants to be and the irrepressible need for mediation which seems inherent in human nature.

4. SOME CONSEQUENCES OF THE ONENESS AND TRANSCENDENCE

(a) *In relation to knowledge of God, faith and theology*. The oneness of God is revealed by the Koran, and the monotheistic faith is a gift of God, as the Koran repeats, even if it should also be obvious to sound reason. The Moslem faith is 'supernatural in type': it is believing in God because he has said he is one (*credere Deum Deo*, 'believing in God on God's authority').[6] But there has been a great temptation to treat the Koran's injunctions to use reason as invitations to prove the existence and oneness of God rationally. This would take us closer to the 'God of the philosophers' than to the God of revelation, but it is also to forget the Koran's frequent appeals to the 'mystery' (*ghayb*) of God, which 'human intellects cannot compass' (Kor. 2, 3.255; 20, 110, etc.).

The problem is all the greater in the absence of any real conception of analogy between God and creatures, which leaves no middle ground between univocity and equivocity. If one takes literally the Koranic assertion that 'nothing is like God,' one can say nothing about him in human language. More seriously, God can reveal neither other truths nor himself, since all revelation addressed to human beings takes place in human language. Whether the Koran is created or uncreated was a question which provoked bloody clashes in the early centuries of Islam. The modern discussion about the word of God in human language is barely beginning to be tackled by a few present-day Moslems.[7] Similarly, the role of reason in the interpretation of the Koran, in other words, theology, has been and remains a source of conflict between schools and tendencies, ranging from the literalist Hanbalism, which keeps to the revealed text and easily falls into agnosticism—or anthropomorphism—to the various more or less rationalist schools: mo'tazilism, developed ash'arism and recent reformism, which rarely avoid tautology. Reason is still looking for acceptance in Islam.[8]

(b) *In relation to God's action on human beings and the world*, the ever-present insistence on oneness tends to make God, the only being which exists in the true sense, (who 'exists by essence'), the only genuine agent. In extreme cases, the human person is no more than the site of God's action: 'He created you, you and your actions' (Kor. 37, 96 interpreted). Similarly, human causality and secondary causes in general, and even the ontological solidity of the creature, tend to disappear. This is what has been called Moslem atomism or occasionalism, an idea which is well known and repeated rather too much, because the main schools of Moslem theology in fact reject this model. For the mo'tazilites the human being is really the 'creator' of his or her actions, indeed the sole creator; for the great ash'arites, such as Ghazâlî, God and the human being are both causes of a human action, God as the universal creator and the human being as the 'acquirer' of his or her action. In the view of the reformists, such as M. 'Abduh (died 1905), the human being performs the action and God, if need be, 'completes' it. Modern Islam is massively voluntarist, not to say 'horizontalist'.

In relation to social life, the Moslem city, the sole sovereignty of God leads to a rejection of a separation between temporal and spiritual (*dîn* and *dunyâ*), and so to State religion (*dîn al-dawla*). This again is well known and often repeated, as if it were the political doctrine natural to the Koran and Islam. Theorists (in the West) even see in this the paradigm case of the connection monotheism-theocracy-intolerance. They forget that, historically, Christianity's trinitarian monotheism has not always prevented theocracy and intolerance. They also seem unaware of the fact that, in the history of Islam, whole sectors of civilisation and culture have had no hesitation in claiming and exercising genuine autonomy in relation to the religious authorities. For example, many 'Moslem' countries today are officially secular (Turkey, Syria, South Yemen and sub-Saharan countries which are nevertheless 90% Moslem, such as Niger) or secular in practice. Intellectuals in Islam have been arguing for the separation of State and religion for 60 years, and their numbers are increasing. Finally, the autonomy of temporal structures can legitimately claim support from a reinterpretation of the Koran.[9]

A final point which should be mentioned, which there is no room to expand, is perhaps the most important consequence of Moslem monotheism, its effect on religious and spiritual life. The stress on the absolute oneness of God makes him appear as the only being who really exists; every creature is essentially 'decaying' (*fânin*, Kor. 55, 26–27). The believer is centred, polarised, on that unique reality. The minimum implication of this is the attitude of adoration, of 'surrender of self to God' (*islâm*), the observance of the revealed law, a deep sense of dependence, of being 'a beggar before one's Lord' (*al-faqîr ilâ Rabbihi*), as Moslems, both rich and poor, like to sign themselves. Historically, this sense that the creature is nothing and God all, the *todo y nada* of St John of the Cross, has been the point of departure for the Moslem mystics, the sufis. Their journey towards God has taken many forms, from the unsatisfied love of God of Rabi'a (eighth century), the sense of the indwelling of God in the mystic and the union in love expressed by Hallâj (ninth-tenth centuries), to the radical and paradoxical inversion of God's transcendence in Ibn 'Arabî (thirteenth century) and his school of pantheistic monotheism, which had a considerable influence on the religious brotherhoods: if God is the only being who exists, everything that exists is God. 'The universe is like ice, and God the water from which the ice is formed (Jîlî, fifteenth century). But it is preferable to stay with the eminent sense of transcendent unity expressed in these two poems of Hallâj:

Make me profess your oneness truly, beloved One,
For no (human) path will lead me there.
I am a reality and for the Real (God) that reality is a reality
Clothed in his essence. No more separation between us.
See the shining brightness of the dawn grow stronger,
Sparkling in the dazzling light.

Guide of ecstatics, glorious king, I know that you are transcendent.
I proclaim you as greater than all the glorifications of those who say
'Glory to you,' greater than all the concepts of those who conceptualise
you. My God, you know that I am powerless to offer you the thanks you
deserve. Come into me to thank yourself. This is the true thanksgiving.
There is no other.

5. MOSLEM MONOTHEISM AND CHRISTIAN MONOTHEISM

From as early as the Koran, Christianity is presented as unfaithful to the
monotheism preached by Jesus (3, 51; 4, 172; 5, 116–117). In particular, the
Christians adore three gods (4, 171; 5, 73), namely, God, Jesus—and Mary
(5, 116). They say that Jesus is God ('God is the Messiah, the son of Mary'
(5, 17.72)) or the son of God (9, 30). The Koran also denies the crucifixion of
Jesus (4, 157–158). Christians also, in the Koran and in the Moslem tradition
from the beginning to our own time, are regarded either as infidels (*kuffâr*) or
'associators' (*mushrikûn*) or as 'people of the scripture' (*ahl al-kitâb*) and, in
virtue of this, heirs of the monotheistic tradition deriving from the earlier
prophets. There are few Moslem theologians who recognise, like Ghazâlî, that
Christianity is indeed a monotheism, though different from Moslem
monotheism. This recognition is beginning to grow now, notably in Islamo-
Christian encounters.

Christian Islamicists since Louis Massignon (1863–1962) have thought and
written a great deal about these Koranic denials of the Christian mysteries.[10] It
can be seen, of course, that as they appear in the Koran the Christian mysteries
are very different from their Christian definitions: a triad of gods, a deified
man, and so on. In this respect the Koranic denials have to do with incorrect
formulations which we condemn as much as the Koran, not with the real
mysteries. But to stop there would be to betray the faith of both sides. The
truth is that these denials of mysteries, whether in their incorrect or their true
formulation, derive from a fundamentally different conception of the unity
and transcendence of God.

Koranic and Moslem monotheism is the affirmation of the oneness of God, not only externally (no other god), but also internally. It is the conception of a God who is indivisible, indissociable (*samad*, Kor. 112, 2), 'solid casting', in modern industrial terminology. Moslem theologians devoted a wealth of ingenuity to reconcile this internal oneness of God with the multiplicity of divine 'names and attributes', which might or might not be identical with the divine essence.[11] And when they became familiar, as they did quite soon, with the Christian Arab theologians' explanations in terms of person (*uqnûm*, from the Syriac *gnômâ*) and nature (*tabî'a* or *kiyân*, from *kiyânâ*), they nonetheless rejected them as incompatible with true (Moslem) monotheism.

It is the dogma of the incarnation, however, which, in the eyes of Moslems, prejudices the absolute transcendence of the one God. Even with the clarifications of the early Christological councils and theologians, who attempted, more or less successfully, to reconcile the reality of the incarnation with the transcendence of God, the essential difference between Islam and Christianity was to remain. On the one hand, one and the same being cannot be both truly God and truly man; on the other, the unique and transcendent God (the Son) himself is born as a man, suffers, dies and rises.

6. MOSLEM MONOTHEISM AS A CHALLENGE TO CHRISTIAN FAITH

For the Christian faith, the powerful affirmation of the oneness and transcendence of God as understood by Islam for over thirteen centuries, and accepted today by over 800 million Moslems, is a challenge to deepen the understanding and practice of its own monotheism in the aspects it shares and, above all, in the aspects in which it differs from that of Islam.

A possible first step would be to recover, where necessary, and practise the monotheism of Jesus of Nazareth, a true son of Israel, who made his own the *shema' Israël* (Deut. 6:2; Mark 12:29–30 par) and was entirely oriented towards the one God he called his Father and our Father, the Father of all humanity. This is also the movement of liturgical prayer, to the Father, through the Son in the Spirit.[12]

Here it is useful to be aware that some Moslem scholars of today who are quite familiar with work in Christian exegesis and theology find in them a confirmation of the Koranic views, on all but the crucifixion, which is a difficult problem. The 'Jesus of history' did not call himself God or Son of God. He was the obedient servant of whom the Koran speaks and whose admirable message can be received with profit by a Moslem. But the elaborations of the Christian tradition which 'interpret' the life and message of Jesus and gave rise to the New Testament writings, quite apart from those of the councils and theologians, are human work, no doubt worthy of respect, but no less foreign to the Moslem faith than to the message of Jesus. This 'interpretative' tradition does not meet the canon of literal transmission which is the only one recognised by Islam as authentic for the transmission of a prophet's message.[13]

At this point the challenge joins with that of modern criticism, and we all know what havoc that can wreak on a faith nourished on pre-conciliar Catholic theology. There can be few educated and sensitive priests or laity who have not felt the shock-waves. But what is really happening here? We are being forced to abandon bad proofs and forced back on faith in the action of the holy Spirit who has guided the Church from its beginnings to our own day, despite its human obtuseness. May this not be a grace? Never has the expression 'the Christ of faith' seemed to me so justified.

Our faith accepts the witness of the apostles and holds to the tradition of the Church. But every age has its problems, to which the Church has to devote particular attention. The Church of the first centuries had to clarify its doctrine to meet contemporary heresies, and the theologians attempted to penetrate the mysteries by intellect enlightened by faith. But the best theologies of the Trinity and the incarnation will nevertheless always be humble approaches to unfathomable mysteries, as the great theologians of the Trinity, St Augustine and St Thomas Aquinas, were well aware. This should put us on our guard against all scholarly trinitarian or Christological constructions, let alone the constant temptation to 'prove' the Trinity, even without going so far as Hegel's dialectical demonstrations, and encourage us to return to the more modest formulations of scripture.

Similarly, there is traditional Christian language which is best avoided in a Moslem environment; talk of the divinisation of the Christian is one example.[14] The same applies to certain forms of devotional or spiritual life which affect a familiarity with the persons of the Trinity closer to tritheism than to trinitarian monotheism. Conversely, a Christianity reduced to a vague monotheism, not to say a vague theism or even deism, has more to do with the religious instinct than with Christian faith.

At a deeper level, the Moslem challenge to Christian monotheism is one of the best instruments I know for stripping the Christian faith of its accretions. Islam may call itself, justifiably in my view, the 'religion of human nature', but Christianity, despite Tertullian and his 'naturally Christian soul',[15] is certainly not. To believe in God, and therefore in one God, adore him, submit to his will, all that, in a sense, is natural. To believe that God became man, suffered and died depends on faith and on extraordinary grace, even if it is shared by more than a billion people. Here again, Christians have to abandon habits of thought which have come to seem natural, forged as they have been by centuries of Christianity and reinforced in each of us from our cradles, in order to recapture the wonder felt by the first Christians or modern converts. To be more specific, Christian faith is not primarily a slightly different form of monotheism, but the Easter faith. We believe that Jesus, who died on the cross, has risen and entered into the glory of the Father, and is *therefore* the eternal Son of God and himself God, and *therefore* we believe that God is Father, Son and Spirit. Resurrection, incarnation, Trinity: we are a long way from the Moslem faith.

And we must go still further. Islam, from the Koran on, has approached Christianity from its doctrinal, theological side, what Christians say about the oneness of God. Jesus was faithful to monotheism; Christians are unfaithful to it.[16] But we cannot let the Moslems define the terms of the debate. Christianity is not first and foremost a doctrine, but a life in accordance with the Gospel. It has even been said that Jesus had no theology of his own about God the Father; he took the theology of his Jewish environment, but he made it operate in a different way.[17] The fathers said that 'theology' is for 'economy'.[18] The sole purpose of doctrine is to ensure correctness of life. Jesus is the Son of God because he is the perfect revealer of the universal Father, so that human beings may live as a family, as children of the Father through the Son in the Spirit. It is significant that the Koran reduces the Gospel (*injîl*) to a word or a scripture which 'came down on Jesus', whose content was wholly doctrinal. The real message of the Gospel is not denied, but ignored.

Finally, the difference within God the Trinity must be taken seriously as a warning against any monolithic or exclusive view of salvation.[19] We must honestly admit that Christianity has rarely escaped from such a view in the past 20 centuries.[20] The time has come to recognise all religions as so many ways for human beings to work out their relationship with God, and even so many refractions of the word of God in human history. We must do this without in any way minimising the uniqueness of the word of God in Jesus Christ, but rather by focusing more sharply on its detail, its real originality. This uniqueness has no absoluteness or exclusivity. And what doubt can there be that a message about God such as is transmitted by the Koran and Islam has a divine origin and an eminent place in the revelation of monotheism? Theological attempts to take account of this phenomenon have multiplied in recent years, though space prevents us from doing more than note them here.[21]

7. A MUTUAL CHALLENGE?

The question mark after this heading refers, not to the principle, but to its practice. Christian faith's challenge to the Moslem faith has indeed been presented, from the time of the Koran, as we have indicated, but its result has been a hardening of monotheism and a continuous sequence of increasingly bitter polemics, even when Christian teaching is understood in its authentic form.[22]

There are nevertheless grounds for thinking that trinitarian monotheism may help Moslem monotheism to avoid the twin temptations of arithmetical, tautological oneness and of rationalist deism, by returning to the Koranic, and largely traditional, emphasis on the unfathomable mystery of God: God is unique with a mysterious uniqueness and human beings know of this only what God reveals to them. There are already cases in which this mutual challenge is being effective.

The stress here on the fundamental differences between the two monotheisms, Christian and Moslem, should not be taken as a denial of what is genuinely common to them and distinguishes them, and Judaism, from other world religions. It is a revealed monotheism, a faith based on adoration and witness: 'God alone shall you adore.' This cry of millions of believers is powerful in a world which is multiplying idols, instruments to enslave human beings, golden calves along with gulags. It is in this sense that believers in the one God are members of one family, as the Koran says (49, 10).[23] And if these monotheisms, at least Islam and Christianity, seek to be universal, the competition between these universals should be transposed today from the secular plane of polemical or military confrontation to that of 'rivalry in good works' (Kor. 2, 148; 5, 48), the service of human beings in the name of the one God.

Translated by Francis McDonagh

Notes

1. Louis Massignon *Les Trois prières d'Abraham. I. La Prière sur Ismaël* (Tours 1935) p. 41.
2. Stanislas Breton *Unicité et monothéisme* (Paris 1981) pp. 43–58.
3. See my article 'La Rencontre des théologies' *Lumière et Vie* 163 (July 1983) 63–80. A number of ideas from this article are developed here.
4. See Toufic Fahd *Le Panthéon de l'Arabie centrale à la veille de l'hégire* (Paris 1968).
5. Literally 'according to the original nature *(fitra)*'. The Koranic sense of the word, clearly established by exegetes, refers to Moslem monotheism, the religion of human nature as created by God.
6. This is the central theme of my doctoral thesis *La Foi musulmane selon le Coran* (Rome 1965). See *Proche-Orient Chrétien* (1968) 17–28, 140–146; (1969) 162–193.
7. The pioneers in the recognition of historicality and human mediations in the Koran (F. Rahman, M. Arkoun and others) belong to our own time. See R.C. 'Vers

une nouvelle interprétation du Coran en pays musulman?', in *Studia Missionalia* 20 (1971) 115–139, which now requires updating. The Islamo-Christian Research Group (GRIC), established in 1977, has been studying this problem for five years. Its conclusions will be published shortly. On GRIC, its nature, work and conclusions, see R.C. 'Le GRIC', in *Islamochristiana* 4 (1978), pp. 175–186. The subsequent issues of the same journal report the annual meetings of GRIC. See also *Lumière et Vie* 163 (1983) 81–85. On the general problem, R.C. 'Parole de Dieu et langage humain en christianisme et en islam' in *Islamochristiana* 6 (1980) 33–60.

8. There is a good summary in Mohammed Arkoun *Le Pensée arabe*, series *Que sais-je?*, No 915 (Paris 1975). This point is developed at length in my *Cours de théologie musulmane* (Rome 1975, 2nd ed. 1979), 2 vols duplicated, printed edition planned for the end of 1984.

9. See the important article by Abdelmajid Charfi 'La Sécularisation dans les societés arabo-musulmanes modernes' in *Islamochristiana* 8 (1982) 57–67.

10. See the authors and references in my *Cours* (details above, note 8), 1979 ed. I, pp. 41–42, 48–63; II, 36–40; printed ed., pp. 69–72, 79–116.

11. See my *Cours*, the chapter 'Dieu, son existence et ses attributs'. This is an appropriate place to state my conviction that the only way for Moslems to approach the true meaning of the Trinity is through this reflection on the divine names, despite the difference between the divine persons and the divine names. (References in the chapter of my *Cours* just mentioned.) This was, moreover, the approach of the medieval Christian Arab theologians: see Samir Khalil 'L'Unité absolue de Dieu; regards sur la pensée chrétienne arabe' in *Lumière et Vie*, 163 (1983) 35–48.

12. I shall not here go into the current debate between Christocentrism and theocentrism. See Jean Milet *Dieu ou le Christ? Les conséquences du christocentrisme dans l'Eglise catholique du XVIIe siècle à nos jours* (Paris 1980). However, Christian life in Moslem countries encourages priority for theocentricism.

13. Evidence for this line of thought in the work of GRIC (details above, note 7) on scripture, to be published shortly.

14. Based on 2 Peter 1:4: 'partakers of the divine nature'. Taken literally, this is *shirk*, 'associationism'. The fathers, particularly in the East, use this language frequently, as do the Rhenish mystics, notably Meister Eckhardt. Thomas Aquinas, however, explained that the organism of grace inhered in the soul 'by accidental mode' and not substantially (1a, 2ae., q. 110, art. 2, and 2 & 3). On this see Louis Gardet *Dieu et la destinée de l'homme* (Paris 1967) pp. 103–106.

15. It is significant that Tertullian justifies this expression by the natural human orientation to *monotheism*: see *Apologeticum*, ch. 17 (PL I, 376–377).

16. See the article cited above, note 3.

17. Christian Duquoc 'Jesus, le non-théologien' in *Dieu différent* (Paris 1977) pp. 43–60.

18. Arguing the same point, and on the issue in general, see Paul Aubin *Dieu: Père. Fils, Esprit: Pourquoi les Chrétiens parlent de 'Trinité'?* (Paris 1975).

19. This is the main theme of C. Duquoc, the work cited in note 17, esp. pp. 125–149.

20. See, among other works, my study in progress 'Pour une vision chrétienne du

Coran. I. Les Données historiques' in *Islamochristiana* 8 (1982) 25–55.

21. See my *Cours*, cited in note 8, printed ed., pp. 75–116, and Claude Geffré 'Le Coran, une parole de Dieu différente' in *Lumière et Vie* 163 (1983) 21–32.

22. On this abundant literature, see the exhaustive bibliography, going back to the origins of Islam, in *Islamochristiana* 1 (1975) and subsequent issues, and each annual issue 'Bibliographie du dialogue islamo-chrétien'.

23. This is an extension of the Koranic formula (which refers only to Moslems), but one made today by many Moslems. On this family of faith, see paragraph 5 of the 'GRIC charter', 'Orientations pour un dialogue en vérité', in *Islamochristiana* 4 (1978) 183–186, esp. 185.

PART III

Present-Day Questions

André Dumas

The New Attraction of Neo-Paganism: A Political, Cultural and Spiritual Phenomenon or Epiphenomenon

ACCORDING TO those false prophets that analysts of the future of society so often are, it seemed at one time that the industrialised and urbanised countries at least were inevitably moving towards secularisation. Now, however, we are witnessing many cases of a resurgence and re-establishment of the sacred, so much so that the sparring partner of faith will no longer be an atheism that has become exhausted after a century spent in an all too disappointing exercise of power, but several varieties of neo-paganism that challenge both the nationalist inheritance of the Enlightenment and the Judaeo-Christian faith within which it was secretly and cunningly formed. A tendency is emerging that has decided to use, not the formula 'on the other side of' death resurrection, 'on the other side of' history the Kingdom, 'on the other side of' men and various cultures the one God, but Nietzsche's beloved formula: 'beyond' monotheism and atheism, 'beyond' good and evil, 'beyond' the holiness of God and the desacralisation of the universe, a new sacred sphere in which man can be healed of the effect of all those poisons that are known by such names as egalitarianism and universalism, dualism and totalitarianism. This is a new tendency that is trying to behave as though Jesus and Marx—and I would also add Descartes and Hegel—had never existed, as they say, to our greater misfortune. Returning to paganism therefore has its charms.

It will be obvious straight away that what we have here is a nebula that is difficult to define without magnifying or distorting it. At present it is an epiphenomenon in journalism rather than a genuine cultural phenomenon at the popular level,[1] emerging at a time of revolutionary disillusionment, cultural formalism and spiritual doubt in the West. It is the foam on the troubled but still not uncomfortable sea of our present time, when we can dream, but are not driven to tragedy.

The political aim of this neo-paganism, to which its adherents gave the name of 'the New Right' before that sector became so congested, is to rediscover the healthy principle of both individual and collective human inequalities. It does not simply try to justify these differences, following the current fashion of all political movements, but dares to speak of inequalities, thus coming into conflict with the teaching of Jesus and Marx as well as with that of Descartes and Hegel. 'What we need now, at the end of the present century, is a synthesis of positive aspirations of a kind that have up till now only been provided here and there. This synthesis is tantamount to going beyond the present stage of the human condition. I believe that such a synthesis is possible, but I am not sure whether we will be bold enough to put it into operation. I am afraid that we shall be prevented from achieving it by the egalitarian ideology'.[2]

The encouragement of a free but unequal interplay of man's creative powers is also a political aim of this movement. This should not be confused with the passivity of natural forces. The movement openly praises one of the most profound, but frequently most hidden foundations of pagan antiquity—an acceptance of inequality that always prevented its philosophers from being concerned about the existence of slaves in their society. What is important is the art of living, in periods of enjoyment as well as of self-possession. Equality, which is belied even more in culture than in nature[3] is not regarded as important.

Why, then, is this creative inequality suddenly being praised so much? I think it is in reaction to the disillusionment caused by the revolutions of the past two hundred years that have not achieved what they promised. They promised political equality at the end of the eighteenth century, but have in fact created new social inequalities. Above all they promised economic equality at the beginning of the present century, but have brought about ideological inequality. That is why contemporary neo-pagan thinkers bluntly denounce equality as an apparatus used by those of no ability to dominate the able. Like Nietzsche, these thinkers are politically anti-Christian and opposed to socialism, because they are fundamentally anti-democratic and paganism provides them with suitable letters patent.

The cultural aim of this epiphenomenon is to reinstate all the distinctions that raise each individual and each culture or people to the level of a treasure which would otherwise be lost in the mass. This energetic return to individualism is not of itself opposed to the State, so long as the State confines itself to its narrowly political function and does not interfere in individual values. These neo-pagan thinkers are certainly not liberals in the economic sense of the term, but individualists in the cultural sense. They are aware of the tasks of the political city, but they resist totalitarianism in any form. In this, they seem to me to have inherited the best of ancient paganism and its many and varied ideas, with their great mutual tolerance and frequent syncretism. We should openly recognise that this is attractive to the modern world that has suffered so much from ideological dictatorships.

Finally, the spiritual aim of this movement is to provide men who no longer believe in the messianic promises of Christianity or in the humanistic promises of Marxism and who are conscious of an inner vacuum and do not know to what sacred sphere they should devote themselves with a new devotion.

There are three important consequences to this: the tragic aspect, which is not taken in by illusory kingdoms that are still to come; the mythical aspect, which is rooted in the shadow side of the cosmos, when what ideology demanded is historical translucence; and the mystical aspect, which knows the extent to which the soul is reduced by atheism to the paucity of reason. Here too, it seems to me to be right that paganism should look for antecedents in classical antiquity that is ultimately more orientated towards mystery than towards rationalism. Here too, it is very tempting to take advantage of doctrinal weaknesses to enable vague longings to penetrate. But this neo-pagan tendency is still too much in its infancy for us to want to remember that the Nazi movement began with similar exaltation. I think that it is to the credit of this challenge from anti-monotheism that it is more open, more honest and more admirable than it ever was in Nazi-ism, which disguised its fundamental paganism in a celebration of divine providence and appropriated God and his churches instead of fighting him and denouncing them. These neo-pagans do not look for a concordat. They are directly polemical.

1. TOWARDS A PLURALISM IN HEAVEN AS ON EARTH

The attack against monotheism is very simple. The thesis is that monotheism seeks to prevent the pluralism that is indispensable to human life. Monotheism acts as drastically as a steam-roller, especially when it is based on an election by which one God makes himself known to one people and calls that people to become an example to all others. It seeks to impose one way of truth on the multiplicity of life. Even with the best ethical intentions in the world, it is impelled to reject differences and to prescribe its one way, unlike polytheism, which reflects the multiplicity of peoples, cultures and values that form the rich mosaic of the world and which reproduces in its scintillation the countless movements of the human heart and the unbounded perspectives of the sacred cosmos—this is clear in ancient mythology. Monotheism of every kind passionately seeks perpetual peace that can be achieved by the triumphant monopoly of one religion. Polytheism has no such aim. 'European paganism is based on an antagonistic pluralism of values. Polytheism is the expression of this antagonism, which never results in irreversible antitheses or in a radical dualism, but which is naturally resolved in a harmonious whole'.[4] The polytheism of heaven, then, should provide earth with the opportunity to become an earthly crucible, whereas the monotheisms of heaven have always resulted in wars that were seldom holy.

I would not like to try to use apologetics to refute these attractive arguments, in which various forms of polytheism are given idyllic attributes, although they were frequently imposed by the emperor and were hardly colourful mosaics worthy of respect, while monotheism is regarded as a fateful form of totalitarianism. Other young thinkers, for the most part Jewish, have used apologetics in the opposite sense, maintaining that only monotheism can be a safeguard against totalitarianism and natural, ideological and State idols.[5] The annoying feature of all these arguments is that they aim to establish by apologetics which preclude debate that personal conviction provides inescapable evidence. It is in this way that all apologetics cover their own weakness.

It is important to know whether the link between monotheism and cultural monolithism and between polytheism and cultural pluralism is as real as has been claimed. Let us take two biblical examples: the blessed plurality of the different peoples on earth, in addition to, but not contradicting the election of Abraham (Gen. 10) and the plurality of the many peoples of the world hearing the same Spirit and each speaking in their own tongue at Pentecost (Acts 2:1–13). The reader tends to experience the opposite effect and to think that the oneness of God is always accompanied by the multiplicity and great plurality of creation. The Bible in fact speaks of one God in heaven—one creator, reconciler and redeemer—in order to avoid the risk of raising to the level of that God what is no more than the diversity of the world, of various peoples and cultures and of differences on earth that are not inegalitarian, in order to ensure that the state of non-solitude that God the creator wanted all men to share for their own happiness is respected: 'It is not good that man should be alone' (Gen. 2:18). Would not the effect of an extension of pluralism on earth to a pluralism in heaven be to suggest that religion is only a projective human phenomenon and that the least certain aspect of polytheism is the gods or the God who affirm their existence in it?

2. NIETZSCHE VERSUS MARX

It is hardly possible not to hear the voice of Nietzsche and to be conscious of the suppression of the voice of Marx in this rejection of egalitarianism, the so-called classless society and the atheism of mankind that is said not to be exploited or alienated and this affirmation of polytheistic paganism. However many attempts have been made to bring them together as thinkers who shared a deep suspicion of Christianity, they are, after all, very opposed to each other. I am of the opinion that the real conflict in the modern world is between Nietzsche and Marx, since biblical faith is different from what they denounce. They situate it wrongly—Marx places it in the order of heavenly reward for earthly resignation and Nietzsche in that of the poisonous mediocrity of little people who overturn the true values of life in order to obtain the false values that they desire. In situating it wrongly, then, both Marx and Nietzsche find themselves discussing a caricature. It is as though we were to debate with Stalin instead of with Marx or with an American exponent of social biogenesis instead of with Nietzsche. Indirect encounters in which the same enthusiasm is not shared or in which the chin has to be raised (claiming, for example, that faith is cosmology of evolution or a lyrical expression of life) or the backbone bent (abandoning earth, for example, to the pseudo-scientific laws of Marxism in order to shelter as a Christian in a supernatural end-point beyond death or maintaining that the unconscious is sovereign and cannot be reached, faith in the meantime sheltering in a moralising pseudo-rationalism). Marx and Nietzsche, on the other hand, are totally opposed in one respect, that of the future of man in his loss of the old God of the Judaeo Christian faith. Marx proclaims the definitive establishment of atheism. He was as convinced of this as he was of the definitive victory of the universalism, unfortunately still abstract, of Christianity over paganism. He regarded a return to paganism and even more a return to polytheism as a regression, just as, for him, it would have been a backward step to abandon an urban economy for an earlier village type of society. He had a deep Western and Hegelian conviction that it was impossible to return to stages of history that had been definitively superseded, even if the alternative—socialism or barbarianism—overshadowed the future like a dark cloud preventing the revolution from being automatically guaranteed. He was certain that paganism belonged to the past and atheism to the future.

Nietzsche proclaimed the opposite: that what its adherents believed was free thinking atheism, but what was really only a pettiness prolonged by those who wanted to dominate life that was both wild and tragic with the false values of science, education and pretension belonged to the past. The future, on the other hand, belonged to those who dared to become the carriers of a new sacred structure built on the ruins of the scrupulous and tormenting dualistic rationalism that had begun with Socrates and had become more ponderous with Moses and above all St Paul. The new sacred structure would, Nietzsche believed, be pagan, declaring that 'all those who say "yes" to life, those for whom "God" is a word that expresses the great "yes" to everything, are pagan'.[6] Or as a journalist, always on the look-out for provocative but pleasing news, has said: 'Paganism is not, as is sometimes thought and even said, a negation of the sacred. On the contrary, it postulates that the sacred is within reach of human existence. It should not be confused with atheism or agnosticism, but it rejects the one God who is outside this world and yet jealous and who forbids his creatures all spiritual experience, having man in his relationship with the world as its object. That one God calls on men to know that they are exiles. Paganism, on the other hand, looks for religion in an exalted feeling of fullness here and now. It does not desacralise the world, but, on the contrary, sacralises it. It regards it in the strict sense of the word as sacred'.[7]

The matter is made quite clear, as it were, by antithesis to the biblical statement. God does not exist. Could he exist if his effect were for his word to be dualistic and have an emasculating effect on a world, a cosmos that is his own sacred sphere? Everything here recalls the ancient pagan world, whereas Marx always had difficulty in finding ancestors in antiquity whom he could accept, whether in the materialism of Democritus or in that of Epicurus, both of whose writings were, in spite of everything, too full of gods and respect for the gods.

Nietzsche presents us with the wheel of fate revolving and coming back to the same point after all modern man's mistaken attempts to make diminutive steps forward. This destiny is not, however, a horrible repetition of a horrible past.[8] It is venerable and even lovable in accordance with the great paradox of the *amor fati* that is clear about the new beginning and tragic with regard to the absence of an end. Paganism, then, is the beauty and the melancholy of the unchanging silence of the world and wisdom for whoever has had the courage to abandon the deceptive foolishness of theological hope. Marx laicised it into hope and the neo-paganism inspired by Nietzsche went into mourning for it for ever.

3. BUT IS THERE A NEW SACRED SPHERE, OR A NIHILISM OF LIFE?

It is difficult not to resort to apologetics when one undertakes to criticise what is outside one's own domain, because it is not easy to see why one should have to accept a messianism of doctrines that reject, perhaps for their own sake, all messianism. All the same, we have to dare to insult the insolent and to interpret, in the announcer, the tempter who is not sure of his own resources.

The sacred sphere is never new, especially when it is cosmic, mythical and even mystical. It is a very old message which is trying to express itself again at a time when science has succeeded, at least as much as faith, in penetrating the mist that surrounds it in the same way that museums of art and popular traditions are set up in countries where folklore is no longer a living reality. For there to be a sacred sphere, there must be a veneration that is experienced and not decreed. One cannot help thinking in such cases that pagan polytheism is only being restored as a protest against that cultural totalitarianism that is believed to be the inevitable consequence of all monotheism. It is not so much a question of venerating the new or old gods as of loosening the iron collar of what Manuel de Diequez has called the monotheistic idol.[9] It is also significant that the word 'sacred' is used and not the word 'gods'. It is more a question of aesthetics, beauty, play and pleasure and innocence and leaping up than of waiting in fear and trembling, as though there were a real mystery to be venerated on which our life and death depended.

Nietzsche was more ambitious than these fashionable neo-pagans in believing that he was and wanting to be the bringer of a fifth gospel, that of the eternal return of all things and of the justice of midday. It is in fact, to use Nietzsche's own language, a question of a 'reactive' thought and not of a founding or announcing thought. It reacts to various ideo-theological monolithisms by the apologetics of individualism, which does not, however, misconstrue the function of the State as the sovereign authority of the nation. It is what Alain de Benoist has, following countless others, called 'a third life between the octopus State of the socialists and the night-watcher State of the liberals'.[10] This discourse is quite commonplace and it is difficult to see why it should be overloaded with scholarly references to every religious form that has preceded or has remained outside biblical messianism, of which Marxism is only one laicised and socialised form.

The secret of this neo-paganism seems to me to be that it needs a myth to replace faith and ideology. A myth has the effect of rooting the individual in the cosmos and of giving him both eternity and a taste of everyday experience without needing to promise him a better future or to evangelise him on the basis of a revelation. The successful concept now is culture, not religious faith or political ideology, but it is a word that would still be too human if it did not appear with a sacred aureole with the pagan courage to examine the secret aspects of the world. De Benoist's tone is peremptory: 'We have to ask ourselves the urgent question why the twentieth century has not created any great political ideology. It would be simply very narrow-minded to apply now systems inherited from the eighteenth and nineteenth centuries. The results would be mediocre if not disastrous'.[11] The theoretical substructure is also both disparate and meagre and I wonder whether what lies behind this call to a new sacred sphere is no more than a nihilism of life, especially when no word comes to it from anywhere else but from itself and it has abandoned the task of making its own last judgment of the course of universal history. Unless being a modern pagan really means being haunted by the nihilism that threatened man and his culture? Who tells us, moreover, that the ancient world did not experience its art of living more from a dull consciousness of the world's muteness than from a veneration of its sacred lustre?

4. IDEOLOGIES, ATTRACTIONS AND CONVICTIONS

We have lived for a long time in the land of those ideologies that are trying not to charm, but to indoctrinate and mobilise us. That is why they cannot endure joking, but can with an easy conscience punish every deviation, however minimal it may be, that has affected the mass of the people and the moral legitimacy of their political representatives.

Those ideologies have, however, been stripped bare today. They appear as they have become, even if they have not always been like that, in other words, as means of power over the masses that are more dispossessed than truly represented. The heavy bludgeon of propaganda has killed the people's desire to participate. Science can no longer be mobilised at the pleasure of social ideologists. Everything has become more modest, more laicised and more wholesome, but also of necessity more disillusioned.

It is in these circumstances that the need for charm has arisen, that is, the need not to teach but to make oneself attractive and not to influence but to allure. The recipe for charming is well known: one ingredient is an association with dreams about the imaginary, but another is keeping at a distance, so that the magic of not knowing what is remote is not destroyed by a knowledge of what is close. There is in every attempt to charm a journey into the exotic and a visit of the impromptu. In such post-ideological and undoubtedly also post-Christian conditions—although this cultural expression strikes me as a meaningless hold-all—the attraction of recalling paganism seems normal, as does the choice on the part of the 'New Right' of literary symbols not from among the analysts, the witnesses, the prophets, the militants or the farm labourers, but from among such charmers as, in the best case, Stendhal.

It is not always wrong to charm in this way. It is taking the trouble to conquer what has not been acquired straight away, especially in the case of the freedom of a spirit, the tastes of a heart or the trust of a body. The charmer knows that he may fail and be left more bruised and empty than pleased and happy. There is in charming an uncertain quest for novelty that is ultimately more moral than the possession of truth and justice. Charm can, however, only be an initial approach. Otherwise, it is soon thrown into disorder because it has not been able to know, love or be loved. Neo-paganism, reacting as it does to the rejection of monotheism, is today only the thought and exercise of charm. It lacks the conviction that might allow it to persuade men that it is to their advantage to replace the oneness of a God who speaks through the pluralism of a world that looks at itself and remains silent. The novelist Jean Cau was preaching against his neo-pagan parish, I think, when he told the story of the children, in a village in the south of France who had forgotten the Church's teaching and the socialists' programme, but who knew the names of the plants and the stars.[12] But his story ends badly with his hero's ecstasy of love, being consumed by fire and committing suicide in a state of exaltation. We cannot play with impunity with the cosmic forces and it is undoubtedly God's vocation to deliver us from these through faith and man's vocation to protect us from them through the work of history.

When neo-paganism is really unleashed, we know that its innocence is in fact cruelty, its abolition of sin is association with the abyss and its contempt for forgiveness is man's destruction. Can we respond to it? The only possible answer is to show how the oneness of God and that alone blesses the multiplicity of the world without either making it uniform or fragmenting it. This question cannot be answered in a single article and here too one must be content simply to charm and not to teach.

Translated by David Smith

Notes

1. It would therefore be completely wrong in my opinion to identify the recent success in the French elections of a traditionalist and xenophobic movement like that led by Le Pen with the confidential writings of an élitist essayist such as Alain de Benoist. It is clear from both his *Vu de droite. Anthologie critique des idées contemporaines* (Paris 1977) and *Comment peut-on etre païen?* (Paris 1981) that such an identification is out of the question. Why, then, should we not recognise that here?

2. Alain de Benoist *Vu de droite*, cited in note 1, at p. 22.

3. Michel Foucault had exactly the same views about antiquity in the last two volumes, published just before his death, of his history of sexuality, *L'Usage des plaisirs* and *Le Souci de soi* (Paris 1984), even though he had throughout his life fought for those excluded from order.

4. Alain de Benoist *Comment peut-on etre païen?*, cited in note 1, p. 203.

5. See Bernard-Henri Levy *Le Testament de Dieu* (Paris 1979).

6. Nietzsche, *L'Antichrist* (French translation Paris 1978) p. 102.

7. Louis Pauwels *Le Droit de parler* (Paris 1981) p. 295.

8. The Czech novelist Kundera has denounced the unbearable weight of thought and existence in his novel *L'Insoutenable légèreté de l'être* (Paris 1984).

9. Manuel de Dieguez *L'Idole monotheiste* (Paris 1982).

10. Interview with Alain de Benoist, 'Les Ordonnances du docteur Droite', in *Le Monde* 18 June 1984.

11. See the above interview.

12. Jean Cau *Le Grand soleil* (Paris 1981).

Joseph Comblin

Monotheism and Popular Religion

THE WORD monotheism does not come from traditional theological language. However, it has crept in surreptitiously while still retaining the ambiguity of its origins. The word comes from the religion of philosophers and has a strong tinge of rationalism. In fact, the word monotheism does not describe the Christian view of God particularly well. If we use the word monotheism at all, we must be prepared to criticise it. Here we give it a simply negative sense: monotheism is the religious system that defends God's uniqueness by fighting against polytheism and idolatry. In fact monotheism is the opposite of polytheism. But is there such a firm opposition in reality as that between the words monotheism and polytheism? It could be that in reality there exists neither monotheism nor polytheism in the strict sense of the terms, but always something between the two. And this something could vary in different religions.

This leads us to popular religion. This is the name we will give the religion really experienced by the Christian people, without distinction of social classes and cultural groups. Here we shall be speaking of the popular Christian religion of Latin America. It is not that different from the religion of the rest of Christianity but is the sort we know best.

Of course this popular religion is not polytheist, despite the systematic accusations of the proselytising Protestant sects and the suspicions of many Catholic intellectuals. All Catholics admit as a matter of course and vigorously profess without any shadow of doubt that there is one single God creator of the universe, even those who practise one of the Afro-American cults like Umbanda, Candomble or Xango or even those who practise spiritualism side by side with their Christianity. In this they are probably at one with the vast majority of peoples to whom polytheism has been attributed.

What is in question is not the supreme principle of the universe, but how communication is made between this supreme principle and ourselves. Moreover this single supreme principle is as much of a problem for Christian orthodoxy as it is for popular religion. But what concerns us here are the objections of popular religion and the way in which it has solved the problem by means of the cult of saints and, in particular, the cult of Mary, the mother of God.

1. ONE SINGLE GOD AND THE CULT OF SAINTS

The single God, as he is thought of and experienced in popular Christianity, leaves two needs unanswered, the need for particularity and the need for intimacy.

(a) Particularity

According to popular religion there is one single God above all creation, the Lord of the universe, who is the same for all nations and all people. He is the God of the whole world. But it is sometimes difficult to have a personal and particular relationship, an intimate relationship with a God who is everybody's God. If he is everybody's God, he is nobody's God. He is not concerned with anyone in particular. This is the problem.

The cult of saints is selective and particular. Everyone has their favourite saint. Moreover we do not choose our saints but certain signs show that it is the saint who has chosen us. Likewise every association, every group, even every parish, every town and every country has its own particular saint.

This relationship with the saint is an alliance. Between the saint and the person or group of people a permanent pact of alliance is made. He or she is my saint and I belong to this saint. We can count on our saint and our saint can count on us.[1] Everyone has their own way of expressing devotion to their saint, as each saint has his or her preferences and particular way of treating each worshipper.

Although the alliance is permanent, it is also possible to make provisional contracts with our saint: to promise favours in exchange for other favours. These contracts are for special circumstances. As well as the permanent alliance, the worshipper turns more spontaneously to his or her saint when particular social, money or health problems arise.

These relations with the saint are eminently personal. They are unique. Moreover they serve to identify people and groups. Such and such a village belongs to this saint and the next to another saint. This association is attached to these saints and that one to those other saints. This enables each association to be absolutely sure of its identity in the midst of a world that is too big. Your saint is your protector. Such and such a saint is my patron. This community has that saint as its patron.

The worshipper has immediate access to his or her patron saint and the approach is completely particular. Contact with the saint is made by a particular image or statue: this statuette is 'my' saint. It stands in its own place in my house or in a particular chapel in a particular place. My saint is this image and not another.

In one parish, for example, there are three images of St Sebastian, one large, one medium and one small. So each group in the parish has its own particular St Sebastian. You may worship the small St Sebastian but be completely indifferent to the large.

Likewise the great saints like Our Lord and the Virgin Mary have many different titles and each title is like a saint in its own right. You can be extremely devoted to Our Lady of Lourdes and completely cold towards Our Lady of Fatima. You can be a fervent missionary of the Sacred Heart and an implacable adversary of Christ the King. Because the relationship is completely different. If the Sacred Heart takes you up, it would be infidelity to run after Christ the King.

Let us note that this phenomenon exists throughout the Catholic Church. The orders and congregations each have their saint, their title of Our Lady and their title of Christ. The Franciscans have the Immaculate Conception, the Dominicans Our Lady of the Rosary, the Carmelites have the Virgin of Mount Carmel, the Salesians Our Lady Help of Christians, the Redemptorists Our Lady of Perpetual Succour and so on. The lay associations attached to these Orders have the same devotions. For their part the parishes are also dedicated to a saint or to the title of a saint, as are the dioceses, countries and countless Catholic organisations.

Here too the saint is completely localised: linked to a particular sanctuary, image or special cult. The saint has his or her own feast day and particular way of celebrating it.

What is interesting is that this religion of the saints corresponds fairly exactly to the religion of the Old Testament. Yahweh behaves like the saint of Israel. Between Yahweh and Israel relations are direct, immediate, selective and particular. Between Yahweh and Israel there is an alliance. Yahweh is the God of Israel and Israel is the people of Yahweh. Between Yahweh and Israel there are contracts: Israel can call upon the name of Yahweh and he has undertaken to help her. Israel can ask for help but in return must offer God what he asks for, keep his Law.

The God of Israel had the unique quality of being both the God of the universe, the creator of all humanity and the particular God of a small nation.

Biblical monotheism did not destroy the particularity and special relationship. On the contrary it exalted it. The particular saint of Israel is so strong that he is Lord of the universe and Israel is the favourite of the king of the whole universe: a nation which shared in his universal kingship. There is no doubt that in this religion as it was experienced, Yahweh was first and foremost 'our' God, the God of our group and our people before he was God of the universe.

With the expansion of Christianity throughout the world, Yahweh underwent a dissociation. He remained God of the universe, but he ceased to be anyone's God in particular, 'our God', 'my God'. Once Christians filled the whole world, being the God of the Christians was no longer a particularity but rather a new form of universality. This is when the need for particularity was felt anew, the need to have a heavenly protector of our own, who knows us in particular and adopts us for his own.

Of course there is Jesus. But he also becomes the Lord of all and he only becomes accessible by means of particular titles. As a rule Catholic people do not address Jesus Christ in general, but Jesus Christ perceived and adopted under a particular title. Jesus in general cannot really be interested in our particularity.

In Latin America the need for particularity was felt from the beginning, much more even than in other Catholic countries. The conquerors brought with them their saints and their devotions and these saints were thought of as bound to favour them. Adopting them meant attaching oneself to the conquerors; adopting their particular gods meant recognising their privileges.

In fact saints and cults appeared among the Indians which were opposed to the conquerors' saints. These gave the conquered their own identity, patronage and protection from the dominators.

The most famous example is the Virgin of Guadalupe, venerated on the hill of Tepeyac, which at that time was one league from the capital but which today has become part of Mexico City and stands almost in its centre.

Herman Cortes brought with him in his luggage the Virgin of Remedies, the protectress of Spaniards, whites and the social élite. In contrast, the Virgin of Guadalupe appeared to an Indian at Tepeyac and it was through the Indian Juan Diego that the Virgin ordered the bishop to build a church on this hill. The hill of Tepeyac was the place where the Indians worshipped Tonantzin, the mother of the gods. From then on the Virgin of Guadalupe of Tepeyac became the symbol of the Indian and half-caste people of Mexico, the Virgin of the conquered and the banner for all popular uprisings. She is still the rallying cry of millions of Mexicans who have gone to the United States to look for work. The Virgin of Guadalupe enabled the Indians to hold their heads high and stand face to face with the gods of the Spaniards. She is the adversary of the Virgin of Remedies.[2]

Another example is Our Lady of Copacabana. At Copacabana on the shore of Lake Titicaca the Indians had a famous sanctuary dating back to before the Incas. There they worshipped the Pachamama, the Earth mother. Here too there arose a sanctuary of Our Lady which became a rallying point for the Indians. The Virgin of Copacabana is celebrated in countless places throughout South America from Ecuador to Chile, wherever the Inca empire once extended. She stands face to face with the saints of the conquerors.[3]

Another example is that of the apostle St Thomas. The Spaniards had waged war on the Moors for centuries in the name of St James. This same St James accompanied their armies to America and ensured that they were victorious. Against St James the defenders of the Indians appealed to St Thomas. Was it not said that St Thomas had evangelised the Indies? Many missionaries believed that they found traces of Thomas's mission in the Americas. This was enough for him to be put forward as the defender of the Indian peoples and thus to become a counter-weight to St James.[4]

If it had not been for these saints, how could the Indians have found a place in Christianity? God, it was said, was the God of all and was thus indifferent to the divisions between human beings. Only the saints could enter into these particularities.

The same went for the Blacks. They too had their groups and associations, thanks to the saints who gave them an identity.

The Virgin of the Blacks in Brazil was Our Lady of the Rosary. After some events which have been reconstructed, it was Our Lady of the Rosary, famous for her victory over the Turks at Lepanto, who was charged with taking on the cause of the Blacks against all the Virgins of the whites.[5] But as well as her, the Black people also counted on the protection of several Black male and female saints: St Benedict, St Iphigenia, St Anthony of Catagerona, St Gonzalez, St Onofre. Even today it is still these saints who enable the Black people to have their place in the Church.

As long as the monotheism of one and the same God and one and the same Jesus Christ for all is accepted as Christian doctrine, what other remedy is there against domination, apart from the saints?

Of course it is possible to wonder whether the God of Christians is as universal as bourgeois theology claims. In the Old Testament he was the particular God of a particular people. The mistake made by the Jews was to believe that God had chosen Israel for its own national qualities. But in fact God had chosen Israel because it was an oppressed people. Jesus was the saviour of the oppressed. In reality the God of Christians is not the God of all but the God of the poor and oppressed. We must recognise this particularity in him, which he never abandoned.[6]

The saints will only cease to be important when God becomes important again. In bourgeois religion God has ceased to be important. He has become as banal as a metaphysical principle. He is no longer of any interest. But he becomes interesting again when he regains his particularity as the defender of the conquered and oppressed.

(b) Intimacy

The God of Christians has become remote and like the universal God worshipped by almost all the peoples of the world. Such monotheism is almost universal. But almost as meaningless as it is universal. For nearly all people the sovereign God is outside the scope of cult and worship. He is recognised but not worshipped or very little. Even the Catholic liturgy has no feast in honour of God the Father: it would be too boring. This universal God is in fact boring.

We feel the need to see, hear, gaze at, touch with our hands, as 1 John 1:1 puts it. Faith needs to touch. Because knowledge of the divine is through the whole body.

Hence the need arises for appearances or manifestations of God, either in people or in objects, which can be seen, heard and touched. The Catholic people sees manifestations of God in certain particular people, perhaps a priest or a missionary. For example the pope is seen as a visible manifestation of the divine and through this great white figure, the mystery of the divine becomes present. This is not a deification of the pope but a perception of the divine through him.

There is also the Eucharist. Traditionally and still today the mass is an epiphany of God. The important thing is to see the host. Then the whole people acclaims it and says: My Lord and my God.

Relics had this role for a long time but the priests have got rid of them. There remain the images which the priests have not yet succeeded in removing, except in bourgeois families. The Protestants have the Bible, which can also be touched and felt as if one were feeling God's body.

Of course Jesus himself was the epiphany of God but he has gone away and he too now needs mediation in order to become familiar. In nearly all the poor houses in the North East of Brazil there is a picture of Father Cicero, who was a country priest who died 50 years ago. He was also the people's adviser for 50 years. He had trouble with his bishop and with Rome, was suspended for many years but none of that counts. The portrait is the presence of Father Cicero in the home and Father Cicero is the presence of the Sacred Heart of Jesus.

God's lack of closeness to human beings is felt all the more strongly because we can only express faith and devotion with our whole body. Thus we need to know where we can find or meet the divine and how we can make contact with it. What can we do for it?

In general in the North East, people do not go to prayers or to mass. They go where there is something to do: carry a cross, build a house, a chapel, a dam. They can only pray with their hands. If there is nothing to do they feel uncomfortable, they feel they are redundant and they stand aside and wait to see if God needs them one day.

God needs no one. It is said that he has all the glory in himself. Well then let him remain alone with his glory. The saints on the other hand are less proud. They are willing to ask for services. They are close, they come near.

2. THE SINGLE GOD AND THE NON-CHRISTIAN RELIGIONS

Nearly all peoples have a certain monotheism and a varied religion, which is more or less rich and scarcely addressed to this single God at all, except in the case of Islam which heavily emphasises its monotheism.

We might wonder whether the popular religions of Asia and Africa have a similar attitude to official Christian monotheism of the twentieth century as that of the traditional Christian countries.[7]

In Africa, for example, there are all kinds of relations with spirits. Are these offensive to the supreme God?

Can we not think of such relations with spirits as a way of sharing in the life of the universe and all its forces, as a kind of sharing in the concert of praise and thanksgiving which the universe offers its Creator?

Religion is first and foremost ritual, bodily expression, the use of the body.[8] It is spectacle and physical exercise, it lies somewhere between gymnastics and theatre. If it associates figures, images, pictures, persons and symbols with the spectacle, can all these be regarded as God's rivals, offensive to God and a rejection of the supreme God?

Here an inevitable question arises: the Christians have fought against all expressions of non-Christian religions for twenty centuries with a ferocity that would not rest until all was destroyed; were they not deceived (in good or bad faith) by Old Testament polemic? In fact when the Jews fought against other religions, what were they protecting? The universal God or their own particular God? Were they defending the God of the universe or their own particular God, the God of their tribes, the God who did not allow them to mix with other nations? Were they not defending their difference against the difference of others?

But we have rejected the difference of the people of Israel, so why should we fight against the differences of each people with its religion? Or is Christianity also one religion among others, fighting for its particularity at the same level as the others?

Over the centuries mission theologians explained the likenesses between the Christian religious system and other religious systems as the cunning of the devil. The Indians had rites which were like Christian rites. The explanation was very simple: it was a stratagem of the devil to deceive these poor Indians. Fortunately the missionaries were even more cunning than the devil and succeeded in unmasking his trickery.

What did this mean? That Christians and non-Christians had religions on the same level: one was true and the others were false. As if God had arbitrarily chosen one system among others deciding that this would be the true one. But why would it be truer if God is the God of all peoples? Can the difference be on the level of religion? If pagan rites offended the God of the universe as idolatrous and superstitious, why did the Christian rites not do so too? Only because God had intervened to say that the latter did not offend his transcendance whereas all the others did?

It is better to conclude that all this biblical polemic is simply irrelevant. It has been superseded by Christianity. It has kept the Christian Church within an ethnocentricity from which it has only recently begun to escape. The Church thought of the missions as Israel thought of proselytism: as propaganda by a whole religious system against other religious systems.[9]

3. MONOTHEISM AND RELIGION AS A FIGHT

In Latin America monotheism was used in three ways to justify the destruction of the people's religion. In the first place it justified the systematic destruction of the traditional religions of the inhabitants of the Americas. This destruction was done in two waves. The first immediately followed the conquest. The missionaries used the secular arm to force the Indians to surrender all their religious objects, which were all publicly burnt. Their temples were pulled down and their clergy persecuted and reduced to clandestinity.[10] And the second time during the first half of the seventeenth century the Catholic clergy made systematic searches in order to eliminate the final remains of 'idolatry'.[11] The whole religious system was simply regarded as the work of the devil and sacrificed to the transcendance of the Christian God.

The second wave of attack was by the Protestant sects who arrived mainly since the end of the last century, convinced that their mission was radically to destroy the paganism of the Catholics. They pursued wth religious hatred all the images and all the manifestations of popular religion, which they denounced as idolatrous.

The third wave came from the Catholic clergy themselves between the years

1945–1965 during the 'modernisation' of the Catholic church. This provoked violent struggles between the iconoclastic priests and the faithful. The priests were usually victorious.

The worrying thing is that the Church, her priests and her missionaries are transformed into combatants and really believe they are doing this work of destruction for the glory of God. Piety and devotion are replaced by violence and destruction. Does this destructive God, in whose name whole cultures are wiped out, become the greatest idol of all, the idol of power denounced by the Puebla Document?[12]

Translated by Dinah Livingstone

Notes

1. See Pedro A. Ribeiro de Oliveira 'O catolicismo do povo' in *Evangelizacǫo e comportamento religioso popular* (Petrópolis 1978) pp. 28–32.

2. See Enrique Dussel *Introducción general a la historia de la Iglesia en America latina* (Salamanca 1983) pp. 571–574.

3. See Enrique Dussel, *ibid.* p. 582–584.

4. See Enrique Dussel, *ibid.* p. 574.

5. See Juliat Scarano *Devocǫo e escravidao* (Brasiliana 357) (Rio de Janeiro, 2nd ed, 1978).

6. See Stanislas Breton *Unité et monothéisme* (Cogitatio fidei 106) (Paris 1981) pp. 61–66.

7. See Aykward Shorter *Théologie chrétienne africaine. Adaptation ou Incarnation* (Cogitatio fidei 105) (Paris 1980) p. 111–3.

8. See R. Panikkar *Le Mystére du culte dans l'hindouisme et le christianisme* (Cogitatio fidei 53) (Paris 1970) pp. 34–37.

9. See, for example, Joseph de Acosta *Histoire naturel Le et morale des Indes occidentales. 1589.* (Paris 1979) pp. 235–287.

10. See Fray Gerónimo de Mendieta *Historia eclesiastica indiana* (Mexico 1971) pp. 226–244 and *passim.*

11. See Manuel Marzal *La Transformación religiosa peruana* (Lima 1983).

12. *Puebla* No. 502.

Gabriel Vahanian

Monotheism and the Critique of Idols Yesterday and Today; or else: Monotheism or the Critique of Idols Yesterday and Today

1. THE WEST AND ITS IDOLS: RELIGIOUS UTOPISM

'THE WORLD needs some kind of utopia', said Alfred Kastler, Nobel prize winner in physics, not so long ago. Anyone who knows how carefully he chooses his words will realise that the word 'utopia' was not used here as casually as one might think. If, therefore, he felt it necessary to adopt this term, it was because he spoke not only as a scientist but also as a humanist concerned about the religious vision of a world which respected the dignity of contemporary man.

But what sort of utopia did he have in mind? To say the least, one would expect a scientist, with his roots deeply embedded in the West and with no fixed ideas about the religious (Christian) tradition which shaped it, to have another view of the utopia the world needs than the caricature of it so often, and sometimes rightly so, conveyed by many authors who are not so much disappointed by the West as subject to an out-of-date view of the West, christendom and religiosity. A view of a world. As if it were out of the question that the world, so much loved by God that He sent His only Son, could ever have been the best of all possible worlds.

But, apart from Orwell, few authors are aware of the fact that Thomas

More, the inventor of the term, wanted through his Utopia with its implicit criticism of contemporary English society to carry his readers along with him without them having to abandon the principles of their political or theological allegiance—on the contrary. So, all he asked for was a simple effort to take language at long last seriously and the best approach was to apply the well-known use of *understatement*. And one should be familiar with this language, rather than being obsessed, weakened or drained by it. Indeed, far from making man superfluous, language adds to man's equipment by supplying him with meaning where there is none. And is this not what Orwell brought out so clearly with his find, the term 'newspeak', which was a stroke of genius in his novel *1984*? And how did he do that? He did it by showing that, in spite of *Big Brother* and a technical efficacy which is the purer and harder because it is imposed in a supple way and without anybody or anything being able to escape its grip, despite *Newspeak* but finally because of Newspeak, there always remains—however one tries to get round it—the ultimate obstacle which cannot be surmounted by even the boldest attempt to dehumanise society and to de-personalise man: language. And, as any language, it swings between two poles, both irreplaceable yet closely linked together: cohesion and coherence. Their interplay has precisely the subtle peculiarity that one term does not absorb the other. This would reduce language to its appearances, to a mechanism so subjected to the ideology which has colonised it that ideology itself has but the appearances of the utopia which it is supposed to embody, but the negation of which it in fact brings about.

Like Christianity, technique readily takes a lot of stick. And so the reader of *1984* quite naturally blames technique for anything he erroneously sees as a deviation from the human element, unaware of the fact that it is precisely through technique—a technique of the human factor—that the humanisation of man operates, and has always done so in so far as the only thing that is alien to man is man.

Yes, technique indeed. Or, if you wish, because of a certain religious concept of the world which happened to be conveyed by the West in general and the Christian tradition in particular; in other words, by a certain kind of religiosity. This religiosity is less centred on the past than on the future, less on antiquity and age-old traditions than on new ways of thinking and acting, however simple-minded this statement may seem. It is less haunted by the course of nature or history, traces of a sacral image of the world, and more at ease with the utopia of a happiness available to all. In short, it is a religiosity which is sensitive to the emancipation of man, created by man and whose concern is man. Whether man descends from the ape or not, he does not just simply descend as one human from another human. He forms one whole with himself as the words of a poem which compose it make the poem a whole and produce something original, and in the case of man this is a matter of the unheard-of. It is a matter even of God, as long as we introduce the reality of the domain of Being into that of language or—which comes to the same—the perspective of the sacred into that of utopia. And so the sacred—where the measure of all things is sometimes God, sometimes man—reaches utopia, where neither God nor man but Christ makes them commensurate. They are *compatible*, and for that very reason one cannot be reduced to the other, but belong to a dialectic, not of identity and difference, but of otherness. This otherness is so radical that Christ, who alone embodies the measure of it, becomes himself the measure of all that is.

The revolution of technique, less industrially and economically orientated than culturally and spiritually because it has its roots in that *verbal* and therefore utopian concept of all reality which includes the religious element, is above all a religious revolution. What it rejects is no more and no less than a mythological discourse about the religious factor seduced by its own rhetoric of the profane and the sacred, the one and the many, what is the same and the different. Technique rejects not the religious factor as such but its paganism (whose naturalism is related to religion as Greek primitivism is to the idea of utopia). And while tolling the bell for paganism, it does the same for all those classical antitheses which not only still echo it but continue to seduce us, such as, on the one hand, theism and atheism, monotheism and polytheism and, on the other, sexism, racism or the struggle of the classes.

St Paul, for whom God and man have meaning only in Christ, had already remarked on this when he wrote to the Galatians: 'There are no more distinctions between Jew and Greek, slave and free, male and female, but all of you are one in Christ Jesus' (Gal. 3:28). Whether the world in need of utopia ignores it or not, we have here a utopian illustration of the Christ-centred concept of both God and man as Paul sets it out.

2. GOD AND IDOL: FROM ANALOGY TO METAPHOR

With regard to both Israel and Greece or, as we would say today, on the 'ecumenical' level and that of the dialogue between religions, Paul frankly adopts a very different line. I shall be told that I impose the reading of it. But it is clear that problems which seem intractable to us, are for him quite simply no longer relevant. His point of view is definite: for both Israel and Greece a new era is opening up, as already pointed to in the apocalyptic trends of the Jews and the gnosis of the Hellenes. There is, however, a difference. The Jews are faced with the problem of passing from a promised land, reserved to the actual descendants of Abraham, to a land of all people. The Greeks have to accept the impossible vision of an earth which belongs to every man (were it not for the obstacle of slavery, something which the Greeks never managed to circumvent).

For Paul, however, every man is Everyman. In Christ. Through him every man, if he is Everyman, is then the very condition of that God who, without Christ, would only be a view of the mind. 'For', as Paul says, 'if the dead are not raised, Christ has not been raised. And . . . your faith is in vain' (1 Cor. 15:16–17). Indeed, at Easter the last word does not belong to nature or history. It belongs to God, and that God in whom man could not believe and whose reality he could not maintain except in so far as, abashed by language, he speaks (Rom. 10:8–10), and by the same token also questions all he can imagine God to be on earth as in heaven.[1] If therefore, however little man adores him, there is no God who does not become an idol, there is also no idol which does not drop its mask, however little man speaks. The dividing line passes no more between theism and atheism than it does between polytheism and monotheism. It passes between God and the idol. Between iconoclasm and idolatry. It passes where the word is an iconoclasm, not of the image, but of silence, and where therefore the imaginary is an iconoclasm of what is real while the real becomes an iconoclasm of the imaginary. Where there is metaphor rather than analogy. And where the metaphor of the Word transcends and overturns all those analogies of being which hardly rise above the level of onomatopoeia, that sort of *newspeak* at the level of the body. Is it then astonishing that under such conditions we should be less afraid of Nietzsche than of Artaud whose purpose it is to 'destroy the metaphor in order to revive onomatopoeia'.[2]

The distance between analogy and metaphor is of the same order as that between being and language, myth and technique, or the sacred and utopia. Or that between the religions of salvation which abounded at the origin of Christianity (as they do again nowadays where it is failing) and the biblical concept of faith as eschatologically oriented existence. The technical revolution lies in the same perspective. That is why, being eminently religious, it is a revolution of language by language, not to destroy it, whatever contrary insinuations may have been made against it.

It is true that, at first sight, one may be upset by the binary aspect of technical language. But nothing prevents us from seeing just here the proof that it resists any reduction and refutes this by fighting against it, not from the outside but from within. It puts man with his back to the wall and forces him to choose like someone without excuses and without an alibi. Or else . . . or else . . . : there is an alternative which makes a man who chooses be what he is when he is not and not be what in fact he is. Simultaneously a sinner and justified, but never less and less of a sinner and more and more justified as was formerly given to understand by a substantialism still imbued with the sacred.

And so technique's imagination, far from doing away with language, has to proceed via language, just as what is real, far from avoiding language or making it lie, promulgates its *veri-fication*.

Nor does it matter whether the language has a natural or a supernatural origin. Thanks to the fiction of language, to language itself and its power of fiction, incommensurates and incompatibles, the imaginary and the real become commensurate and compatible, one with the other. And, as we have said about God and man, they are commensurate and compatible through Christ. Man surpasses man, and God the idol man makes of Him as soon as he has to worship Him, whether as Jew or as Greek, as Christian or non-Christian. Whether man tends or likes to bring God down to the level of an idol, it certainly happens. But this is rather a lack of imagination, the lack of imagination that fails to understand that language and man live by pushing back their respective boundaries.

This is because the difference between God and idol is not evident. So little evident in fact that even the new creature, which is man in Christ, has to be warned against confusing them (1 John 5:21). And this is at God's cost, a God who is the God of the living and not of the dead. At the cost of language which has no more a real word for God and God alone (and not simply *sola scriptura* or even *sola fide*) than a geodesic dome, unlike a tent, has a pillar. And this can only express, not what God is or is not, but this otherness so that those who have ears hear and yet believe and those who have eyes can see and yet believe. It is an otherness which no mirror can express or reflect. And so Jesus says that whoever sees him sees the Father. And what he thus puts clearly before us is not some kind of fusion with God but the fact that the possibility of confusing God and idol may be necessary but is not inevitable.

Two observations here. The first concerns idolatry: it is not the monopoly of polytheism or atheism and so can be equally at ease in monotheism, above all when monotheism rests on the dichotomy of being and non-being, of the profane and the sacred, of the beginning and the end. A dichotomy the articulation of which finds its climax in making language incapable of saying anything whatever until, with Artaud, it is sacrificed on the altar of onomatopoeia.

The second observation is concerned with God: if He has no other reality than that verbal condition of Christ in whom the Word took flesh, then the critique of idolatry must begin with the critique of language and of the dualisms which ruin it and the construction of the alibi of which can only result in the violence done to the language. This violence is not always brought about by non-believers. *Credo quia absurdum* is no less injurious to language than such rents it makes between body and soul, spirit and flesh, or word and image: all such dualisms are less sanctioned by a *sacrificium intellectus* than by a sacrifice of language, that supreme invalidation of man perpetrated as if, in order to speak of God it would be enough to reduce man to silence. As Pilate claimed when he felt forced to ask: 'What is truth?' and then left the high-priests to carry through the ultimate sacrifice. And it seems that neither they can see what is at stake on Good Friday, which is less the impotence of God in the silence of men than the impotence of the idol confronted with the Word.

3. CHRIST: IDOL OR GOD

The great lesson of classical Christology is that language resists idolatry. One says the same thing when one maintains that the only approach to God is through Christ. But it is also clear that using speech does not save one from idolatry. In the same way it does not follow that all christocentrism is free from idolatry. And this is not merely a matter of those who are inclined to see Jesus as the idol of the Christians. But this holds, and above all, for the New Testament which asserts that there is no other approach to God except through Christ simply to combat idolatry, and, for that very reason, gives us to understand that, without God, Jesus himself would equally be but an idol. It is not as if the Christian tradition were not aware of this warning. It may have even been too much so, to the point of subordinating Christology to theology by, one might say, reducing the latter to the former, and all this, of course, in an attempt to establish an intellectual equilibrium that was very unstable. In the end one might say of tradition that it swings between a Christocentric theology and a theist, or even deist, Christocentrism, if it is not, as in certain contemporary circles, clearly atheistic. We all know the slogan: only a Christian can be an atheist. There is nothing strange about this since, if the two terms of any classical duality complement each other, they end up by cancelling each other out. But this is not the main point.

To be brief but at the same time to point out the essential, I would say that, for classical Christianity, the trend has usually been to see Christology and anthropology as the two foci of an ellipse built up by theology. This is contrary to the New Testament which, at least as I see it, would turn theology and anthropology into the two foci of an ellipse which would be Christology. And again, I would add, contrary to contemporary thinking which has slid from the area of being to that of language, and has been led to tackle the problem of God clearly in another way than before. Charles Hartshorne wrote: 'The question of divinity is so fundamental that even the basic rules of our language must either require or exclude God . . . This is the choice—all else is talk.'

Would theology perhaps have become again the queen of the sciences? And of sciences totally emancipated from the tutelage of the Church, so that theology, too, would be free or almost? Why not? This would amount to admitting that it is not so much God who is the problem today (in spite of appearances) but a certain (religious) view of the world, even if it implied that Jesus would hamper the dialogue with some scientific thinking which today is rather keen on theocentrism,[3] or with non-Christian religions[4] or even with some of the themes of theology. For the rest, in so far as Christianity is concerned, the debate would have a chance of taking place on a terrain which suited its postulate of the faith as—eschatic—existence or of the religious factor seen rather as something utopian than as a soteriological quest of being. We should not forget that throughout the Bible theology implies a certain concept of man, which it starts from (as a basis, so to say in the chemical sense of the term): iconoclasm of the gods as much as of God, Adam is no more related to some Mother-Goddess or some divine nature than he is an emanation of God. And if, on the other hand, the virgin-birth does not flatter a kind of male chauvinism, it does not prevent Jesus, the new Adam, born of Mary, from being truly human.

So there remains an iconoclastic principle, wholly motivated by a (christic) concept of God and of man, which has nothing to fear from a dialogue with contemporary science or world religions but which one should not sell off under the pretext of 'religious' solidarity. What in any case we have, or should have, in common with the other religions, is technique. Faced with technique it is more important than ever to maintain Christ's paschal challenge to any claim to the effect that 'Silence or the Cry would be higher or more profound than the Word'.[5] Let us remember St Augustine. It is really because he had identified the demarcation line which runs less between God and man than between God and the idol, that he could write: 'Aut quid dicit aliquis, cum de te dicit? Et vae tacentibus de te; quoniam loquaces muti sunt.' Augustine clearly was on the right lines of the biblical tradition which is less directed against images than against the (muzzling) of speech. The Ark of the Covenant is the opposite of the pagan arches, it is empty, like a screen:[6] it contains no image to represent God, but 'embodies' on tablets that word through which God allied himself with his people. It is because of this word that the Bible, in the name of God, pleads against the silence of man (Ps. 8), just as in the name of man it pleads against the silence of the gods, if not against the silence of God (Abraham at Sodom, Job). Thus, centuries later, when Pascal, held by the vision of a new world, wondered whether he could overcome the fright with which it seized him, it was less because he was afraid of a world emancipated from Christian tutelage than that he sensed that this emancipation might be at the expense of a world which up till then could only be filled by the glory of God. What Pascal was afraid of was the idea of a 'world of things' which could assert itself by escaping from the 'world of words' by a vast sell-out of language.[7] He is afraid of the image of a world which would make one forget the essential: if the dividing line runs between God and the idol, it is because it runs between the word and silence (or the cry) rather than between the word and the image. God speaks, the idol is dumb.

Being one with man, God is one with language. He is its reason (logos), not its alibi. The metaphor, not the analogue. So much so that, with the incarnation, one passes from a logic of the names of God to the logic of the Word, and, from then on, 'every tongue should acclaim Jesus Christ as Lord, to the glory of God the Father' (Phil. 2:11).

The idol, on the other hand, consists in the hailing of language from a distance, its dissimulation by the mask of an analogy which is alien to it to the degree in which, since it does not bear on the verb but on the noun, its anchorage lies in some way outside the language. Lacan has said: 'Analogy is not metaphor',[8] which, as he observed elsewhere, 'lies at the precise point where sense is made in non-sense'.[9] In spite of the non-sense. Thus creation arises in spite of the primal chaos, I would almost say, of nature; or redemption in spite of history. Like any mask, analogy only reveals what it dissimulates. Like the screen the metaphor, if it does not turn into a mere cliché, gets into the background so that language may come to the fore. But this language must consequently imply the need to critise itself.[10] For, in so far as any icon is verbal, it is *ipso facto* iconoclastic.

But that is also the reason why 'language, the essential instrument and mediation through which man expresses and examines himself, that instrument of action and disalienation, becomes alienating and alienated . . . It becomes reified, the limit of alienation . . . It becomes hardened and falls outside the living word'. And it is really all this which Samuel Beckett illustrates better than Nietzsche when, in *Waiting for Godot*, Lucky works himself up in the famous tirade where exactly, riddled with clichés, the metaphor of the Word is eclipsed by a language of analogy which swings towards onomatopoeia, even to a paganism of Christian make-up which, for that very reason, is no less a contradiction in the terms.[11]

Which is anyway the case of all paganisms, including neo-paganism. At least in the West where, whatever the situation, the religious element implies the necessity of its own demythologisation with the same logic as language implies its own critique. Where the critique of the religious factor, if, as Marx says, it must precede any critique, must necessarily deal with the religious element. This is for two reasons. First of all, because the secularisation of religion always comes about through the emergence of a new type of religiosity, not through the abolition of religion, which is the illusion of all illusions. Feuerbach felt this when he admitted that today's atheism made the bed for tomorrow's religion. Secondly, because, to be effective, any secularisation of religion has to be necessarily linked with the process of the desacralisation of the world. This works in favour of another paradigm than the sacral paradigm of the religious factor, that of utopia. This utopia, desacralising in principle, is linked with the paradigm of a promised land, a cosmos, a city of God, even a terrestrial city. That not only biblical faith but also the religious factor demands the necessity of its own demythologisation, as Marx again intuited when he observed that the strength of religion corresponded in fact to a weakness of the technical order faced with a nature which was fatal and even hostile to man.[12]

4. FROM PAGANISM TO TECHNIQUE: THE UTOPIAN ICONOCLASM OF THE FAITH

If Christianity is out of date, so is paganism. If returning to nature is an illusion, returning to the sacred is but a myth, tenacious and as prolific as the ivy. It stops you speaking and saves you from believing. And yet, this is not what should disturb us.

What should disturb us is the rout of Christianity and its spiritual and geographical Balkanisation. What is disturbing is the bad conscience with which Christianity refuses to face the rise of technique although this technique derives, albeit indirectly, from its concept of faith as eschatic existence, in other words, from its utopian concept of the religious element. It is disturbing that Christianity is quite willing to invest in local cultures (African, for instance) and even in various areas of an anthropological, sociological or economic order (feminism, the North–South debate), but it baulks at the idea of investing in a technical civilisation (as in the past it turned its back on the industrial revolution, betraying its mission and alienating the proletariat). Whether the world of technique is the best of all worlds or not, it is nevertheless this world which God loved so much that he bestowed the gift of his only Son on it. It is disturbing that by now drawing the consequences of the cultural vocation which animated Christianity in the course of the centuries, one remains attached to the presuppositions of an ossified spirituality beset by categories and ways of thinking which the technical mentality rejects, the more so as it has inherited them. Fundamentally utopian, this mentality appeals to an understanding of human reality which can in no way be compared to the 'myth of man' so highly praised by paganism, and the memory of which continues to haunt a kind of Christianity still marked by a nostalgia of the sacred. That is what is really disturbing, and it is not lacking in irony, were it only because, in the matter of the faith's cultural engagement, the lesson of

Christianity seems to have been better understood by outsiders than by those who profess it.

Let us look at the nineteenth century. Christianity then wavered between a rather smug modernism or liberalism and a pietistic romanticism or historicism which are no less smug, at least in retrospect. And while the theologians, seeming to rediscover the idea of the kingdom of God, are still at the stage of thinking of the world of economics and labour in terms of the family as the more or less natural unit, it was Marx who looked further and higher and banked on technique: for him it represented the 'royal road to utopia',[13] which means the overturning of an order claimed to be natural in favour of an order that is, at long last, social.

That under these circumstances the thought of some contemporary theologians is still pegged to a conception of nature which derives from the sacred—let that be. But we are astonished that someone like Paul Tillich is still annoyed by it. Wondering about the rise of utopianism which is characteristic of our time, he writes: 'Religion has almost forgotten its vertical upsurge and has devoted its strength to the horizontal element. It has supported an increasing utopianism instead of rectifying it.'[14] No doubt, Tillich admits that utopia is an integral part of religion. This does not prevent a non-believer, Francis Jeanson, from accounting better for the dynamics of Christianity by seeing in it quite frankly 'the negation of the sacred' and the ultimate consecration of a totally different order, that of grace.[15] Or again it is Merleau-Ponty who astonishes us when he writes: 'For at least twenty centuries Europe and a large part of the world have rejected vertical transcendence, and it is therefore rather exaggerated to forget that Christianity is, among other things, the recognition of a mystery in the relations between God and man which consists precisely in that the Christian God does not want anything like a vertical subordination.' Man, at long last, does not become an adult through the death of God, but through the risen Christ. There, there is neither from on high or from below, nor before or after, nor already or not yet. Because God 'is not simply a principle of which we are the consequences, or a will of which we are the instruments, or even a model of which human values would only be a reflection, it looks as if God is impotent without us, and Christ shows that God would not be wholly God if He did not embrace the condition of man.' In so far as transcendence is concerned, it 'no longer hangs over man: man becomes in some strange way the privileged bearer of it.'[16] The erosion of the supernatural does not affect transcendence: it liberates it. Just as faith liberates language instead of locking it up.

For the rest, and in so far as I am concerned, any idea of verticality or horizontality smells of the stake. It points to a closed universe, a language constructed for representation or anamnesis, and which has not been broken in to the anticipation or invention of a new, unpublished word, the unheard aspect of the Word.

Because faith, at least as understood by Christianity, aims neither at totality nor universality—those banal expressions of a sacral dualism—but at the pleroma: when Christ is all in all the practice of human reality reaches its wholeness, while still remaining the proof of God's radical otherness. It is so radical that, today, like yesterday, the unbeliever who lives in each man (particularly after twenty centuries of Christianity) is sufficiently so to say: I believe, help me in my lack of belief!

But how can he say it if Christianity, still haunted by a decadent soteriologism and fixed in its past and its sacralism, exhausts itself by wanting to present the grace of God and His glory as the appanage of a dead language, a myth of man?

Translated by Theo Weston

Notes

1. See 1 Cor. 8:5–6: 'And even if there were things called gods, either in the sky or on earth—where there certainly seem to be 'gods' and 'lords' in plenty—still for us there is one God, the Father, from whom all things come and for whom we exist; and there is one Lord, Jesus Christ, through whom all things come and through whom we exist.'

2. Jacques Derrida *L'Ecriture et la différence* (Paris) p. 282: See p. 275: 'It is the metaphor which Artaud wants to destroy'.

3. See J. Milet *Dieu et le Christ* (Paris 1980); F. L. Baumer *Religion and the Rise of Scepticism* (New York 1960); J. W. L. Sullivan *The Limitations of Science* (New York 1933); K. Jaspers *Origine et sens de l'histoire* (Paris 1954).

4. W. C. Smith *Towards a World Theology* (Philadelphia 1981); M. Boutin, C. Davis, N. King 'Trois approches récentes dans l'étude des religions' in *Science et Esprit* XXXV/3 (1983) 325–351.

5. H. Lefebvre *Introduction à la modernité* (Paris 1962) p. 177.

6. See Y. Kaufman in *Great Ages. Ideas of the Jewish People* ed. Schwartz (New York n.d.) p. 27.

7. J. Lacan *Ecrits* (Paris 1966) p. 276.

8. *Ibid* pp. 262 and 508.

9. J. Derrida, the work cited in note 2, p. 416.

10. H. Lefebvre, the work cited in note 5, p. 176.

11. S. Beckett *En attendant Godot* (Paris 1952) p. 71.

12. See K. Axelos pp. 158 and 294.

13. D. Bell *The Winding Passage* (New York 1980) p. 19.
14. P. Tillich *La Dimension oubliée* (Paris 1969) p. 74.
15. F. Jeanson *La Foi d'un incroyant* (Paris 1963) p. 123.
16. M. Merleau-Ponty *Signes* (Paris 1960) p. 88.

Contributors

ROBERT CASPAR, WF, born in 1923 in Bourg-la-Reine, near Paris, is a White Father. He has a degree in Arabic and a doctorate in theology (Gregorian University, 1965). He was an expert on Islam at the Second Vatican Council and a consultor to the Secretariat for Non-Christians from 1965 to 1972 and a member of the Commission for Islam. Since 1958 he has been professor of Moslem theology and mysticism at the Pontifical Institute for Arab and Islamic Studies in Rome (PISAI, formerly IPEAI), and since 1970 parish priest of Monastir and Mahdia, Tunisia. In addition to about 150 articles on Moslem theology and mysticism, the Islamic-Christian dialogue and the theological approaches of Islam and Christianity, Professor Caspar has produced a *Cours de théologie musulmane* (Manouba, Tunisia 1959, new ed. PISAI 1975, 1979) 2 vols (duplicated); a revised printed edition is due at the end of 1984; and *Cours de mystique musulmane*, PISAI, 1968 (duplicated).

JOSEPH COMBLIN was born in Brussels in 1923 and ordained in 1947. He has been in Latin America since 1958, particularly in Brazil and Chile, but has also been professor at the University of Louvain. His recent works include *O tempo de acao* (1982) (English and Spanish translations in preparation); *Jesus Cristo e sua missao* (Short course of theology, vol. 1) (1983); *O clamor dos oprimidos. O clamor de Jesus* (1984).

ETIENNE CORNÉLIS was born in 1915 at Costakker, Belgium. He successively gained degrees in mathematics at the Free University of Brussels and in oriental history and literature at the University of Liège and a doctorate in theology at the Dominican theological faculty of Le Saulchoir (with a thesis on the cosmological foundations of the eschatology of Origen). Until his retirement he taught philosophy and history of religions in the Faculty of Theology of Nijmegen University and was for ten years professor of the theology of non-Christian religions in the Faculty of Theology of the Institut Catholique in Paris. Among his publications are *La Libération de l'homme dans les religions non chrétiennes, Valeurs chrétiennes de religions non chrétiennes* and, in collaboration with A. Leonard, *La Gnose éternelle*. He has contributed articles to numerous journals.

ANDRÉ DUMAS is a pastor and a professor of moral theology and philosophy in the Faculty of Protestant Theology of Paris. He studied philosophy and theology at Montpellier, Paris and Basle. He was a member of the CIMADE team working in internment camps in the south of France in 1941 and 1942. He was the general secretary of the French Federation des Associations chrétiennes d'étudiants (1943–1949), a pastor of the Reformed Church at Pau (1949–1956) and Protestant chaplain at the University of Strasbourg (1956–1961). Since 1961, he has been teaching in Paris. His publications include Le Contrôle de la naissance (1965), Une Théologie de la réalité. Dietrich Bonhoeffer (1968), Croire et douter. Saint Paul (1971), Prospective et prophétie (1972), Théologies politiques et vie de l'Eglise (1977), Nommer Dieu (1980), Cent prières possibles (1982) and L'Amour et la mort au cinéma (1983).

CHRISTIAN DUQUOC, OP, was born in 1926 at Nantes and was ordained to the priesthood in 1953. He studied at the Dominican house of studies at Leysse, France, at the University of Fribourg, Switzerland, at Le Saulchoir, France, and at the Biblical School of Jerusalem, gaining a doctorate of theology and the diploma of the latter institution. He teaches dogmatic theology at the Lyons Faculty of Theology and is a member of the editorial board of Lumière et Vie. His works include Christologie (two volumes, 1972); Jésus, homme libre (1973), Dieu différent (1977).

BERNHARD LANG was born in 1946 in Stuttgart (Germany) and ordained priest in 1973. He studied theology, oriental archaeology and ethnology at Tübingen, Münster, Jerusalem (Ecole biblique), Paris and London, and holds higher degrees from Tübingen and Freiburg im Breisgau. He is Professor of Old Testament Studies at the Gutenberg University, Mainz, West Germany. His publications include: Frau Weisheit (1975), Kein Aufstand in Jerusalem (1978), Wie wird man Prophet in Israel? (1980), Ezechiel (1981), Monotheism and the Prophetic Minority (1983), Das tanzende Wort (1984). He is editor of the International Zeitschriftenschau für Bibelwissenschaft und Grenzgebiete/International Review of Biblical Studies.

MICHEL MESLIN, born in Paris in 1926, is an Agrégé de l'Université and Docteur ès Lettres, and is professor of comparative history of religions in the University of Paris-Sorbonne, where he heads the Département de Sciences des Religions. His many publications include numerous articles in specialist journals and several books on early Christianity and its cultural context (Les Ariens d'Occident (1967); Le Christianisme dans l'empire romain (1970); L'Homme romain, essai d'anthropologie (1978). His Pour une Science des

Religions (1973) attempts to define the modes of scientific analysis of the sacred from the point of view of religious anthropology. He has recently completed *Le Merveilleux ou l'imaginaire et les croyances en occident*, to be published in October 1984.

JÜRGEN MOLTMANN, a member of the Evangelical Reformed Church, was born in 1926 in Hamburg and studied at Göttingen, where he obtained his doctorate and his *Habilitation*. From 1958 to 1963 he was professor at the Kirchliche Hochschule, Wuppertal, from 1963 to 1967 professor of systematic theology at Bonn University, and is currently professor of systematic theology at Tübingen University. He is chairman of the Society for Protestant Theology, and his works include: *Prädestination und Perseveranz* (1961), *Theologie der Hoffnung* ([11]1978, ET Theology of Hope), *Perspektiven der Theologie* (1968, ET *Hope and Planning*), *Der Mensch* ([4]1979), *Die ersten Freigelassenen der Schöpfung* ([5]1976), *Der gekreuzigte Gott* ([4]1980, ET *The Crucified God*), *Kirche in der Kraft des Geistes* (1975, ET *The Church in the Power of the Spirit*), *Zukunft der Schöpfung* (1977, ET *The Future of Creation*), *Trinität und Reich Gottes* (1980, ET *The Trinity and the Kingdom of God*).

GIUSEPPE RUGGIERI was born in 1940 and teaches fundamental theology at the Theological Studium of Catania. He belongs to the Institute of Religious Knowledge of Bologna, and edits the Review *Cristianesimo nella storia*. His recent published works include *La compagnia della fede. Linee di teologia fondamentale* (1980) and contributions to a study of Erik Peterson and 'monotheism as a political problem', and *La necessità dell'inutile; fede e politica* (1982).

GABRIEL VAHANIAN was born in Marseilles, studied theology in Paris and Princeton, is a doctor in theology and a professor at the Université des Sciences Humaines at Strasbourg after having lectured at Princeton and Syracuse where he founded the school of Graduate Studies in Religion. He has taken part in the President's Commission for the study of Ethical Problems in Biomedical Research (Washington, 1982). He is the author of *The Death of God* (1961); *Wait Without Idols* (1964); *No Other God* (1966); *La Condition de Dieu* (1970); *Kultur ohne Gott?* (1973); *Dieu et l'utopie* (1977).

CONCILIUM 1983

NEW RELIGIOUS MOVEMENTS

LITURGY: A CREATIVE TRADITION

MARTYRDOM TODAY

CHURCH AND PEACE

INDIFFERENCE TO RELIGION

THEOLOGY AND COSMOLOGY

THE ECUMENICAL COUNCIL AND THE CHURCH CONSTITUTION

MARY IN THE CHURCHES

JOB AND THE SILENCE OF GOD

TWENTY YEARS OF CONCILIUM— RETROSPECT AND PROSPECT

All back issues are still in print: available from bookshops (price £3.75) or direct from the publisher (£3.85/US$7.45/Can$8.55 including postage and packing).

T. & T. CLARK LTD, 36 GEORGE STREET, EDINBURGH EH2 2LQ, SCOTLAND

CONCILIUM

All back issues are still in print: available from bookshops (price £3.75) or direct from the publisher (£3.85/US$7.45/Can$8.55 including postage and packing).

T. & T. CLARK LIMITED
36 George Street, Edinburgh EH2 2LQ, Scotland

CONCILIUM 1984

DIFFERENT THEOLOGIES, COMMON RESPONSIBILITY

Edited by Claude Geffre, Gustavo Gutierrez and Virgil Elizondo   171

THE ETHICS OF LIBERATION—THE LIBERATION OF ETHICS

Edited by Dietmar Mieth and Jacques Pohier   172

THE SEXUAL REVOLUTION

Edited by Gregory Baum and John Coleman   173

THE TRANSMISSION OF FAITH TO THE NEXT GENERATION

Edited by Virgil Elizondo and Norbert Greinacher   174

THE HOLOCAUST AS INTERRUPTION

Edited by Elisabeth Fiorenza and David Tracy   175

LA IGLESIA POPULAR: BETWEEN FEAR AND HOPE

Edited by Leonardo Boff and Virgil Elizondo   176

All back issues are still in print: available from bookshops (price £3.75) or direct from the publisher (£3.85/US$7.45/Can$8.55 including postage and packing).

T. & T. CLARK LTD, 36 GEORGE STREET, EDINBURGH EH2 2LQ, SCOTLAND